31 WAYS

of

INFLUENCE

Compiled by Dr. Derashay Zorn

For information about special discounts for bulk purchase, contact the sales department at **sales@divine-order.org**

Designed by D' Technology

Published by:
D.O.R.M. International Publishing
A Christian Publisher located in Atlanta, Georgia (USA)
Visit our website at **www.derashayzorn.com**
Printed in the United States of America
First Edition: August 2019
10 9 8 7 6 5 4 3 2 1
Library of Congress Cataloging-in-Publication Data

Dr. Derashay Worthen-Zorn
31 Ways of Influence / Dr. Derashay Worthen-Zorn – 1st ed.
ISBN-13: 978-0-9862493-3-4
ISBN-10: 0 986249335

DEDICATION

This book is dedicated to every woman in the world. It is our vision to let you know that you are tailor-made by God for such a time as this to do good works within the earth. He has an unmeasurable love for you. By birthright, you are designed to be an influencer. Through this project, we stand with you to break every stereotype that has been placed upon you which have formed a false identity. Collectively, we rise as the Daughters of Zion in purpose, power, permission, prosperity. We know you are called to impact nations, and we couldn't setback another second without seeing you placed in your rightful position. We are calling forth the virtuous woman within you.

Know you are H.E.R!

You are virtuous.
You are that woman that the world needs to see shine.
You are a woman of noble character.
You are that woman who knows how to invest wisely.
You are fearfully and wonderfully made.
You are that woman with many entrepreneurship endeavors.
You are that woman who generates multiple streams of income.
You are that woman of confidence.
You are the woman whose voice is needed in the earth.
You are that woman with good merchandise.
You are more than enough.

You are a Proverbs 31 Woman!

Get Your Free Resources

A comprehensive package of exclusive resources come with this book as a free bonus. There's also a free online course designed to provide additional guidance. To be sure you get the most out of this book, download all the extras and access the companion course at the link below:

http://bit.ly/31waysofInfluence

Table of Contents

ACKNOWLEDGMENTS

I want to first give honor and thanks to God for trusting me with this book and every project associated with it. It has been such an honor to have my steps ordered by you.

I want to express gratitude to my co-authors who caught the vision and ran with it. Your collaboration with this project made it unique and just what God ordered for His people. Each of your portions are vital to this journey so that God can bring healing to a sick world. You are special in the sight of God, and He is going to take you to great places.

I want to thank Denise Walker, founder and chief editor of Armor of Hope Writing Services, for your commitment to making this project shine with a spirit of excellence.

I would also like to thank every individual who purchases this book. You are bringing it to life.

31 WAYS

of

INFLUENCE

Compiled by Dr. Derashay Zorn

INVEST IN YOUR FUTURE
Dr. Derashay Zorn

---

*She considers a field and buys it; from her profits
she plants a vineyard.*
Proverbs 31:16

Success, success, success, and more success; everyone desires it. This is the chatter we consistently hear. An individual craving to become successful is a part of our DNA as children of God. He designed us to be successful, just like Abraham, Joshua, King David, the Proverbs 31 Woman, Madam C. J. Walker, Oprah, Helen Gurley Brown, and so many more. Now, let me clarify. Success is not based upon your economic or social status. It's based upon you passionately loving what you do, where you are, and the direction in which you are going. It brings about peace as you freely live in being who God has designed you to be. I just only mentioned the names of individuals you may be familiar with as they were or considered to be successful in the eyes of the world and others successful in the Lord. Everyone has the desire to be successful in some form or fashion. However, success doesn't just happen. The craving for it is not enough for the transformation of success to happen in your life.

"YOUR WILLINGNESS TO INVEST IN YOURSELF EMPOWERS OTHERS TO INVEST IN YOU"
-DR. DERASHAY ZORN

There is a road that drives a visionary beyond their passion of becoming successful to the destination of manifesting it. Investment is the key that differentiates those that desire success from those that acquire it. "Faith without works is dead," according to James 2:17, and it is going to take work to obtain success. Your level of success is a direct correlation to the level of work you put into becoming successful. I believe the Proverbs 31 Woman understood that very well. As we read about her, we can see that she was a doer of what she believed. She was success-driven. That's why she was careful to consider the fields that she bought. She wanted to make sure that there was a (ROI) return on her investment.

A wise investor needs to know their return on investment (ROI) to ensure they are investing in something profitable. Knowing that one has a

1

favorable return on your investment is what keeps every investor invested. A return on investment is the ratio of gained or lost on the investment you have made. Any investment we make in our purpose will have a gain of 100% and keep us in the green. Yes, we get to live in that abundance of life Christ has given unto us. Every investment that we make out of God's plan for our lives shall be a profit loss, and we shall be in the red and enslaved to bondage with 100% loss. It is time that we truly consider the investments we make, as they determine the level of success we will acquire. Also, make notation that the yielded return on our investments is not always in the form of money.

We cannot begin to make prosperous investments like the woman in Proverbs 31 until we are willing to believe and trust God's plan for our lives and our identity in Christ Jesus. The woman in this scripture was confident in her decision because she accepted her God-ordained purpose. It was not predicated on others but only her choice to trust in God. When we doubt ourselves and are double-minded, we miss out on opportunities to grow and prosper. I believe that this woman's investment did not start at the consideration and purchase of this field. She was an investor way before this point in time. I chose to believe that she took a chance and invested in herself even before others would. That's why she could show up unapologetically and make the type of power moves that impacted her family, finances, friends, and faith. We can see through the text the results of her investing within God's vision for her life.

Have you pondered how she was able to evaluate the field successfully? She had to have learned the skill set necessary to appropriately assess and consider the worth of the field. It could have come through her investment in some form of educational endeavor or the hard price of trial and error. But eventually, she got to a place where she was able to invest wisely.

This woman also acquired the vineyard with her own money. She used the finances she received from her previous business ventures. She made her own money to invest so that her family asset could increase. She didn't wait on others to invest in her worth. The woman believed in what she had to offer and made it profitable for her family and others. The wealth of this woman was already on the inside of her. She just had to trust in the abilities that God had given her to generate wealth. It's the same thing that He has given all of us according to Deuteronomy 8:18. As she invested in her abilities, her return on her investment was profitable as it yielded exceeding great rewards.

Now, let's talk about how we can shift from desiring success to investing and acquiring our dreams of success.

Success, like everything in life, has principles that we must live by to acquire it. To be successful in life, we must follow the laws of investing in ourselves, marriages, families, relationships, ministries, businesses, etc. Invest means to use, give, or devote (time, talent, treasures.), as for a purpose or to achieve something. There are three currencies we must use to invest in our success. We must spend our time, talent, and treasure to acquire success in any endeavor. These are the three-precious commodities we must invest in becoming successful. Your time, talent, and treasures cannot be used independently because it will keep you from reaching the success level of your real potential. Let's observe them independently so that we can understand how they collectively yield a prosperous reward.

Invest Your TIME Wisely

Your time is the number one factor that contributes to your success. Look at how the proverbs woman utilize her time in the text. It took her time to consider which field was worth purchasing so that she can have a return on it. She didn't just pick whatever she wanted. She took the time to investigate it and made sure it aligned with her vision. Not only should your activities be aligned with your vision, but it also must be done in the right season Ecclesiastes 3:1 states, "There is a time for everything, and a season for every activity under heaven:" Are you doing the right activity and the right time in its appropriate season? If you are not willing to invest your time, no other investment would matter.

You can optimize your time by prioritizing how you use it. Scheduling activities that move you closer to your goal will keep you from being busy and missing your next destination. Don't forget to leave time on your schedule for unexpected activities and keep your appointment with success.

ALIGN YOUR ACTIVITIES WITH THE SEASON SO YOU CAN YIELD THE REWARDS.
-DR. DERASHAY ZORN

Cultivate Your TALENTS

Out talents must be cultivated if we desire to master them. What we don't cultivate cannot grow. Therefore, you must start using what you got so you won't lose it. Our skills can be sharpened and enhance through hands-on training, working what we already have learned, or acquiring personal and professional development.

Your current skill level is enough to get you started. So, get started, with evaluation, and adjust as you go. The more you use what you have, the better you will become. Do not hesitate to go back to school, hire a life or business coach to help sharpen your current skills and develop those skills that are dormant. Remember, in the parable of the talents, those who used them received an ROI of twice as much.

It is evident that the Proverbs 31 Woman was like those who utilized their talents as she received the rewards of her investment. She had resources to use from a previous business transaction, where she utilized her gifts. We must cultivate what we have so we can gain more. The world tells us that our gifts will make room for us and place us among kings. The king cannot take notice of a gift that is absent in the earth.

"So, he who had received five talents came and brought five other talents, saying, 'Lord, you delivered to me five talents; look, I have gained five more talents besides them.'" Matthew 25:20 (NKJV)

Invest your TREASURE

Invest your finances in your promise as a promissory note that you shall acquire it.

One of the greatest things you can ever do for yourself is to put a seed in the ground for your success so that you may obtain the harvest. You should be the first person to invest in your future. It paints a picture that you believe in you and gives others the courage to take the risk and invest in you. If you are not willing to take a chance on yourself, it is impossible to think that someone else will. Go out and purchase the necessary things to get you headed down the road to success

Consider this portion of the text where it says she buys the field. This means that she did a business transaction. She took her money and invested in her promise and purpose. She was not looking for a field for no reason. She was intentional with how she was spending her time. This woman was so studious that she wasn't going to waste her time, talent, and treasures on anything that didn't align with her vision and yielding a return on her investment in some form. Abraham invested in the land of Canaan when he purchased the burial plot for his wife, Sarah. He even paid more then what it was worth. Why? Because he knew that one day the entire land would belong to his descendants.

INVEST YOUR FINANCES IN YOUR PROMISE AS A PROMISSORY NOTE THAT YOU SHALL ACQUIRE IT.
-DR. DERASHAY ZORN

Then Isaac sowed in that land, and reaped in the same year a hundredfold; and the LORD blessed him. Genesis 26:12 (NKJV)

SUPPLICATION

Dear God,

I thank you for being faithful in my life. As an awesome Father, you have made sure that I lack nothing to be successful. According to Deuteronomy 8:18, you have given me the ability to generate wealth, in which I am eternally grateful. I desire to produce that in which you have placed with me and I need your help to train me on how to invest in your promise and my purpose in your plan so that your word can manifest. I repent for every place I made investments in my life in the name of Jesus. I thank you for the shift in my heart and mind that they may align with your words for my life.

Today, I crucify my flesh to old habits and ways that have hindered my abilities to invest successfully in the name of Jesus. I thank you for the power in the blood of Jesus to purify. You are my hope, light, and salvation in who I will trust. No longer will I lean on my own understanding but trust in you with all my heart. Like the steps of a righteous man are ordered by you, I will be careful to acknowledge you in all my ways so you can direct my path to opportunities of purpose, promise, and prosperity in Jesus name.

I thank you for the wisdom to utilize my time, talents, and treasures appropriately, that they may no longer be misused or abused. I thank you for the harvest that will manifest in my life through every action of faith that I display. Your love and patience are beyond comprehension. Nothing can truly compare to it. Surely you have kept me for such a time as this so that you can get the glory. I thank you that I was created for a good work that will touch the lives of others. I praise your name that the principles of the virtuous woman are within me. As I move in your purpose for my life, every attribute will be active within the earth, as I pour my life out as a drink offering for your glory. I exalt you on high and praise your holy name for destroying every alter of hinderance and the development of excellent habits. I thank you that everything my hand touches shall prosper, and my feet tread upon shall be given unto me. In the Majestic name of Jesus. Amen, Amen, and Amen

AFFIRMATION

I have the ability to generate wealth.
I am a wealth generator.
I will invest my time wisely.
I am a wise investor.
I shall yield the fruit of my labor.
I will invest in my promise.

I will no longer waste my resources.
I am a good steward.
I am coachable.
I am profitable.
Everything I touch shall prosper.

APPLICATION

Invest in Your Vision

What is your purpose: _____

Knowing the answer to this question is essential to everything you do. It is the vehicle that will align your activities with the plan for God for your life. It will enhance your level of investment as it becomes the determining factor in how you invest your time, talent, and treasures. And what you put in is determines what you get out. Identify ways that you can invest in your purpose

Time

How much time do you spend within 24 hours, 1 week, or 1 month working on your purpose? 24 hours _____1 week _____1 month _____

If you do not know, go and download a time tracker app and begin to monitor how you spend your time or schedule time each day to spend during something working toward your purpose. What you don't track you can't measure.

Talents

What type of activities and how much time do you put into cultivating your talents?

Activities	Time
_____	_____
_____	_____

Treasure

How are you using your money to support your vision?_____
_____

Develop a list of resources that you need to help you in fulfilling your vision. Each month make a goal to check off or save toward one of those items.

Items needed	Completion Target Date	Completed On

Write a declaration on how you will hold yourself accountable when it comes to investing in your promises.

ABOUT THE AUTHOR

Kingdom Strategist, Blueprint Builder, and Spiritual Midwife, **Dr. Derashay Zorn** is an international business coach and expert in the art of **unleashing purpose, developing dreams, and expanding untapped potentials within individuals, corporations, and ministries.** Her passion for information technology has led her to obtain a Master of Science in Information System Management which equipped her to **specialize in analyzing, developing and managing systems to birth or expand individuals and entities into the next dimension of kingdom implementation.**

Derashay equips mankind globally as the Founder of the **Kingdom Influencers Network, In The Church™ TV & Radio Broadcast, Divine Order Restoration Ministries (D.O.R.M) International, Kingdom Strategist Firm, Women of Influence Magazine, (D.O.R.M) Publishing** and many other entrepreneurship endeavors that equip mankind globally. Through, her global brands **Kingdom Strategies University® & School of Authorpreneur®**, she teaches others **how to maximize their potential and monetize their gifts and talents** as a critical vehicle for fulfilling their purpose, making a significant impact and branding influence that can instantly and beautifully change the world. Her books and workbook titled **"Abortions In the Church: Divine Strategies to Spiritual Deliverance" & Meant for My Good: Being Developed In The Midst of the Disaster** is helping others overcome and give birth to their purpose, visions, and dreams. She is a wife, mother, pastor, entrepreneur; consultant, empowerment speaker, mentor, and friend.

Her philosophy is **"A critical tool for self-development is learning how to cultivate, build and release others into their destinies."**

CONTACT INFORMATION

Email Address: info@derashayzorn.com

Website: www.derashayzorn.com

SOCIAL MEDIA

Twitter: @kbstrategist

Facebook Page: @kingdomstrategist

Instagram: @kingdomstrategist

WHY HE CAME
Dr. Dawn L. Cooper

*Favour is deceitful, and beauty is vain: but a
woman that feareth the Lord, she shall be praised.
Proverbs 31: 30*

Relationship was one of the first gifts given to man. In Genesis 1 God created an environment that provided man with everything he needed to live and pronounced to creation that it was very good. Then, He took it a step beyond very good. God said that it was not beneficial for man to be alone, so God reached within Adam and presented him with a woman, Eve – the over and beyond very good.

God feels so strongly about relationships that it was one of the first gifts He gave man. It is true that God created the world for man and gave him dominion and authority over every living thing, but a gift solely to assist and benefit man specifically was the woman – relationship.

It is in the garden that we get a glimpse of a pure and impure relationship with God. In the pure relationship we see that everything was open and nothing hidden between Adam, Eve and God. We see total dependence on God. We see everything working in harmony for the good of the other. No killing and no ill will against another (human or beast), everything was at peace. When sin entered the world, the purest of relationships became impure. Now, Adam and Eve felt the need to hide from God, cover themselves, and blamed others for their own ill actions. The lack of trust in God and the desire to be on the same level as God put a breach in the relationship.

The all-knowing God, in His infinite wisdom, had already put a plan in place to repair broken relationships. However, before we get to His ultimate plan of restoration, we have to look at the components of a relationship. The foundation of any relationship is communication and no relationship could ever exist without it – whether vocal, through actions, or by presence. The one thing that brought everything on this earth into existence was communication – God's spoken Word. And the one thing that keeps it in place is relationship.

One day I was walking along the ocean shoreline and I stopped and looked out over the water. As far as my eye could see, there was nothing but water. I asked God what keeps the waters from spilling out onto the land. He responded that it was His spoken Word. I began to ponder His response and found myself honoring the waters for their obedience to God and longing for the same relationship with Him.

THERE ARE TWO THINGS THAT DETERMINE HOW AND WHY WE FORM RELATIONSHIPS – DESIRE AND TRUST.

Unlike the waters, I have a free will. And as much as I desire to have this relationship, there is also a force I deal with that fights to the contrary. As I sought the Lord on this, I came to understand how relationships are established and what drives them. There are two things that determine how and why we form relationships – desire and trust.

Looking back on my 25+ year relationship with God, there have been many times I have not felt close to Him. I felt something missing in our relationship. I lost my desire to get up early and spend time with Him, walk and meditate with Him, or read the Word of God to get direction from Him. What happened? I didn't feel close to God because my desire for Him had seemingly diminished which resulted in what felt like a more distant relationship with Him.

God answered my prayers but not the way I was expecting. As much as I tried to keep to my normal "God" routine, there was still a disconnect. One day as I sat on my back-patio meditating, God told me that He was not about quotas and check marks. I had relegated our relationship to certain times and places, if I did each, then everything was okay. He showed me that my communication with Him during my drive home was beneficial because I found myself praying for my day, interceding for loved ones, and taking in God's glory through nature. I was now listening to the audio Bible before bed which helped me get direction from God as He ushered me into a restful sleep. Finally, I was not playing worship music at home as much, but in a silent environment I was listening and conversing with God.

God showed me that He was there in all those places. Since my life was changing, so did my mode of communication and times with God. After receiving this revelation, I was more intentional and God-focused during these moments. We must keep in mind that we all experience changes, as I was looking for God in the same places and at the same times, He revealed to me new ways to reach Him and learn of Him. Our relationship became richer as a result.

Because our lives are ever changing, so are our desires. This impacts our relationships greatly with parents, friends, family and God. As we grow our needs change. I don't expect me and my sister's relationship to continue in the same capacity it did when we were young. Through many seasons our communication, our expectations from one another, and our overall relationship underwent changes. Why would a relationship with God be any different?

When I look at the life of Rahab in Joshua Chapter 2, I see a perfect example of how desires and trust can change and how it can result into lasting relationships. Rahab was a prostitute in her town who hid two of God's men that had come to spy out the town with plans to overtake it. She heard of the miraculous power of God and how He had delivered His people from the hand of their enemies. So, when the soldiers of her town came to her door to capture God's men, she sent them another way. Rahab's desire had changed – she now desired the protection of God. Her desire to please men intimately had changed to desiring to please God solely. This was the start of a beautiful relationship with our God as she was loved, protected, and honored, not only by the Hebrew nation, but the all-powerful and loving God.

God longs to have that same relationship with us. Many believe that God put on flesh to die for our sins on the cross. But the cross was never God's final destination. The work of the cross was part of the process, but God's ultimate desire was to put us back into a pure relationship with Him. That occurred when he poured out Himself to the world at the Day of Pentecost. When we receive His Spirit, based on the work of the cross, He sets up residence in us. You are able to hear His voice more clearly. As a result, you are more inclined to follow Him. That's the relationship that God is longing to have with you. Like

GOD IS WAITING FOR YOU.

all relationships, it's a two-way communication. God is waiting for you and until we make the steps to begin and continue to strengthen our relationship with Him, we will never walk in our full purpose.

It is understandable that we may treat our relationship with God differently because He cannot be seen as we see things of this world. However, if you think back on times you stayed up all night talking to men you hoped to marry or the amount of time spent talking on the phone to family and friends, we may get a perspective on how unbalanced we have been in our relationship with God. When we put the same effort into our relationship with God as we do our relationships with people, we begin to see more characteristics of the Proverbs 31 woman manifest in our lives.

I have read Proverbs 31 many times and heard numerous sermons on this chapter. And my mind always goes to how much this woman does – how can any person do all that she did successfully. Recently, God directed me to start looking beyond the services she offered and start focusing on the root behind all she did. We see love, humility, caring, thoughtfulness, willingness, motivation, passion, etc. She was fruitful in all areas of her life because of her relationship with God. No woman could do this without a personal and in-depth relationship with God. It is so much bigger than what she actually did.

Even though this extraordinary woman of Proverbs 31 serves to be an example for all women, she was never named. God saw fit to mention the name of a prostitute, Rahab, or a murder, Jezebel, but not this wonderful woman who exuded the characteristics of God? I believe it is because the author of this book, Solomon, wanted you to understand that the Proverbs 31 woman lies dormant in each of us. YOU are the Proverbs 31 woman! As we submit ourselves to God, more qualities of this woman will unfold because there is untapped potential within us that God is waiting to reveal.

It is not God's desire that we fake at being the Proverbs 31 woman. It is His desire, that through a relationship, we allow Him to shape us into that woman. Many will try to curtail a relationship with God and walk superficially to appear holy, professional, humble, educated, or wealthy missing the concept that there are root behaviors that exude from each of these. If you are truly holy then the world will see sanctification emanating from you. With professionalism, the world will see timeliness. With humility, we see submission revealed. With education, the world will see commitment, and with wealth, we will see giving. People who walk in certain behaviors will exhibit behaviors that align with it. That is why the fake person is only fooling themselves; the rest of us clearly see the truth by the behaviors that manifest from them. Taking the outside-in approach instead of the inside-out approach will prevent your growth in Christ.

I am reminded of the palm tree. In Israel palm trees stand 75 feet with a 30 foot span and 20 foot long leaves. Palm trees are endogens – they grow from the inside. They are extremely useful for food (dates) and their fibers are used for woven ropes, bags, couches, mats, etc. Even in their amazing beauty and usefulness, they continue to grow upward despite the extreme weight on top. The Palm tree's usefulness (external) is matched with its inward growth (relationship). God has honored the palm tree in that it will be with us as we stand before the throne, clothed in white robes holding a palm leaf in our hands waving and crying praises to our God and the Lamb with the elders and angels. (Rev. 7:9-11 paraphrased)

SUPPLICATION

Lord, I want to be more like You. I want a close relationship with You – closer than ever before. And I want it to continue growing all the days of my life. Help me to see that there is never too much of You. As the dear panteth for the water, I want my soul to pant after You. I want to meet You in the secret place. Just You and me. Help me find You Lord. Help me to desire You – to become an extension of You. I promise to yield myself to you, to drop my guard for you, Oh Lord. Give me wisdom on what to remove, change, or realign in my life so any part of You that is lying dormant in me may come alive – yielding a beautiful oneness that will never be matched by any other. In Jesus' name, Amen.

AFFIRMATION

God knows everything. He knows your desires, secrets, and fears. So, why reveal yourself to Him if He already knows? Because God desires a relationship with you. So much so that He died for it. A relationship with you is *Why He Came.*

Every relationship with Him is unique so yours will be tailor made to fit you. You are the only you that will ever exist – don't deny God the opportunity to take up personal and intimate space in your life. He yearns to be a part of you and your daily activities. The greatest part about it is that He makes it easy. He has no expectations of you when you come to Him because He wants the "real" you. If you are angry with Him, tell Him. If you are frustrated because you can't seem to get it right, tell Him. If you feel like giving up because you can't hear His voice, tell Him. If you don't know what to say, tell Him that too. No matter how you come to Him, He will be overjoyed because you took the initial step to establish or strengthen a relationship with Him.

Always know that He formed you, created you, blew life in you, and presented you to the world that He might be glorified through you. Many people will buy this book but only God's chosen will read it – that includes you! So now it is your time to be that living, breathing, walking Proverbs 31 vessel that will change the world! I can't wait to hear your testimony!

APPLICATION

Begin to open up before the Lord. Converse with Him as you would a girlfriend on the phone. Write Him a letter expressing your day, your feelings, or your inhibitions. Making special time for Him is awesome, but don't miss out on the down time you have throughout the day – office breaks, drive time, resting at home. Always be mindful that we were created in the image and likeness of God, so don't be afraid to use all of your emotions in your relationship with God. He can even be quite comical at times. There is no secret formula or step-by-step approach to establishing a richer relationship with Him. But there are must haves in every healthy relationship; communication, honesty, trust, and desire. If you enter the throne room with those components, your relationship with the Most High God will flourish. Arise mighty woman of God – for the Proverbs 31 woman is YOU!

ABOUT THE AUTHOR

Dawn L. Cooper received Salvation on Pentecost Sunday, June 7, 1992. At the age of 18, God drew her to ministries that were governed by the Apostle's doctrine. She is a minister of the Lord and Founder/CEO of Fluent Life.

Dawn is the youngest of three children and was raised in a single-parent home in Cincinnati, Ohio. Growing up in a lower-income neighborhood in Cincinnati had its challenges. It was her drive to succeed that caused her to fight through skin-color isms, poverty, an absent biological father, and various generational sins.

Dawn has served in leadership capacities within local churches and currently serves on the faculty of Kingdom Strategist University. She delivers God's Word globally every third Sunday with Divine Order Restoration Ministries International. In 2017, she became a licensed minister. In 2019, Dawn graduated with her doctorate degree in Theology and Biblical Studies.

Dawn currently resides in Indianapolis, Indiana with her two dogs and enjoys Bible studies, her grandchildren, reading, cruises, and animals. Her favorite scripture is: I Tim. 6:6, "But godliness with contentment is great gain." She is a blessed mother to seven adult children and 12 grandchildren who bring her an abundance of joy!

CONTACT INFORMATION

Email Address: dawnlcooper@YourFluentLife.com

Website: www.YourFluentLife.com

STRETCH ME

Pastor Wanda

Jesus said unto him, Thou shalt love the Lord thy GOD with all thy heart, and with all thy soul, and with all thy mind (Matthew 22:37-39).

L oving God is not just some everyday common undertaking and yet there is a natural inherent spirit-led routine to loving God. It's not a series of "to-do list" performances where upon completion you can say, "Now that I have done such and such," "I love God," but it does involve conduct that strains itself to the fruition of His will for His glory because we love Him.

According to the book of Matthew, chapter 22, verse 37, the God of Glory is to be loved with all our heart, and with all our soul, and with all our mind. Interestingly, the text does not state that we should not kill, or steal, or lie but rather love God. Nestled between a question to Jesus posed by a pharisaical lawyer looking to trap him and a question to the Pharisees posed by Jesus seeking to teach, we find the great commandment mentioned by the lawyer in his question to Jesus. Summed up, the great commandment directs us to love God with everything. In fact, it means we should love Him with all we muster up from your heart, soul, and mind.

Man alone cannot offer to God this "all-type" love described in our text, but man aided and controlled by the Holy Spirit can break through the confines of finiteness and humanity to give God love that involves all his heart, all his soul and all his mind. This all-type love will require a heart that asks the Lord to "stretch me" because the whole extent of what makes me an individual will need to be utilized in my pursuit of loving Him with everything.

BLESS ME AND STRETCH ME

Stretching takes its cue or has its roots in a figure from the Old Testament named Jabez whose name means pain and sorrow. Jabez petitioned the Lord to bless him and bless him indeed. The words he spoke after asking God to bless him indeed are words that have been used by me to author the stretch me concept. What Jabez asked in the next four words in Chronicles is so very instructive and worth examining. They are words that will marvel the eyes of the reader who is hungering and thirsting for righteousness.

BELIEVE IN THE ABUNDANCE THAT IS FOUND IN GOD

Jabez uses the conjunction word "and" to connect the next petition in his prayer to the previous petition to bless him indeed. It's like Jabez said, "AND oh by the way, please do this for me as well." The addendum to part one of his prayer is certain to be delightful delicacies to the weary travelers of this world who desire to love God with everything. So, what did Jabez say next? Let's take a look.

The second part to Jabez's prayer is found in 1 Chronicles 4:10. It states, "Jabez called upon the GOD of Israel, saying, 'Oh that thou wouldest bless me indeed, and enlarge my coast, and that thine hand might be with me, and that thou wouldest keep me from evil, that it may not grieve me!" And God granted him that which he requested. Did you catch it? Jabez asked God to "enlarge my coast." He asked God to broaden his boundaries. He was not content to remain " as is" or be like the status quo but wanted more, so much more. We too can ask God for more. Enlarge means to make larger; increase in extent, bulk, or quantity; add to. We can ask for an increase in the extent of our love for Him. To bulk up our love or build upon what is there.

We can say what I love to say, "stretch me" with smiling hearts. Why? Because we know that we have asked God something that He cannot refuse to give us. Stretch me, stretch me indeed. Video Gamers are on a mission to level up. Similar to Video Gamers as a Christian we can be on a mission in wanting God to stretch our love all the way to the brink. To the end of everything we have to give to Him admiration, adoration and thankfulness for all our merciful God for all He has done, is doing and will do. Bless me so that within the contents of my blessings you stretch me Lord.

We can agree with Jabez. We too want the Lord to bless us indeed. We say amen to Jabez's prayer for the Lord to enlarge his coast but with a little qualifier. Our rewrite might look like this, "Father please look upon my heart as my coast and stretch it in its love for you! Stretch the contents of my heart as far as the east is from the west. From the lowest mountain to the widest valley. Please do not hold back when you use your stretching tool of instruction to train me up as your child." Jabez believed he could be more than the meaning of his name. Remember, his name meant pain and sorrow. He knew that with God all things are possible. Jabez recognized that he could have more. As we examine this text, we see Jabez stepping outside of what some might call a comfort zone. He is not content to be the by-product of a name given to him at birth. God does not change according to Malachi, but sometimes we need to change our attitude or as some might say change our confession or better, our expectancy. Believe in the abundance that is found in God. The Lord Jesus Christ makes a very profound declaration in John 10:10. He professed the "I am come that they might have life, and that they might have it more abundantly." We are not called to live our best lesser life in Him but our best greater life in Him that incorporates expansion in love that is so lavish, lavish enough so that our love cups overflow brimming over with love for God first, last and best. Since Christ came that we might have life and have it more abundantly there is no reason to NOT believe that it would not include stretching us so that we love the Lord with all our hearts, our souls and all our minds. There is no room for lack. As David said in Psalm 23, "The Lord is my Shepherd. I shall not want." We need the sturdy testimony of David to resonate loud and clear in our minds so that we have strong confidence that God will not withhold any good thing from us, especially loving Him with our all. Since the Bible teaches us to love God with everything, we must believe that we can love God with our all and pursue it with everything that we have. Somewhere along the way, Jabez learned that he could be more than his name implied. He perceived the abundance that is in God. He reached outside of himself for expansion. It is our turn to reach outside of ourselves for enlargement as we say, "Lord, stretch me."

Jabez did not just end his prayer with "and enlarge my coast." He followed that request up with another appeal. What did he ask next? He said, "and that thine hand might be with me, and that thou wouldest keep me from evil." He not only asked that his coast be enlarged, but He also desired that God's Mighty Hand would be with him. He did not want to widen his territory without the hand of God being with him. The hand of God with him also signaled the power and guidance of God with him. Jabez wanted to be blessed indeed and be granted an enlarged coast but he did not want the more without God. This point

STRETCH ME FIRST IN YOU AND THEN EVERYWHERE ELSE

is crucial as we review the answer Jesus gave to the lawyer in Matthew 22 when asked what is the great commandment? He told the lawyer the great commandment is to love the Lord with all your heart, soul and mind. If we seek to love God with everything that we can summon up within ourselves without the Hand of God "with us" then we labor in vain. This is a "do it yourself" faith. We should not expect to receive anything from God when we practice a "do it yourself" faith. Spirit raised faith looks beyond this world to the One Who sent His only Begotten Son to die for the world. Spirit grown faith gazes heavenward to the Savior Who finished all that is needed that pertains to our salvation on the Cross. Spirit made faith considers the One Who is the Comforter to be the Great Navigator of this life and dares not go it alone with no Hand of God for the journey. And then there is a faith that is rooted and grounded in the efficiency of God. When we long for God to stretch us first in Him and then everywhere else, it is a longing that is akin to the prayer of Jabez because we too understand that If there is to be real abundance, it is with God. If I am to love God as He intends, it must be with the hand of God with me. Even in our ambition to love the Lord with everything that is within us, it has to be with the guidance of God's hand. Otherwise our seeking is like sound brass and tinkling cymbals. We are just making noise. There is no substance, no weight in desiring God without the Hand of God. It is a longing to be stretched in love in God first and then everywhere else. A yearning to love the Lord with all our heart, with all our soul, and with all our mind. In the words of our Lord Himself, seek ye first the Kingdom of God and all these things will be added.

[This is a "do it yourself" faith. We should not expect to receive anything from God when we practice a "do it yourself" faith. .]

SUPPLICATION

Father, thank you so much for loving us. You love us with an everlasting love that we do not deserve and have not earned. You are always our God who is with us even until the end of the world. You have promised us that You will never leave us nor forsake us. Father, thank you that everything I have ever needed Your Hand has provided. Thank You for being so faithful. I am resting in Your faithfulness as I ask You to create in me a clean heart and renew a right Spirit within me as I come boldly to Your throne of grace expecting You to do what I am unable to do for myself. I so declare my dependency on You. A part from You I cannot love You with all my heart, all my soul and all my mind. I beseech you by Your own tender mercies, by the might of Your Hand to lead me to love you with all my heart, my mind and my soul. I am asking You to do this for me right now. My heart is not harden, and I bow before You, my refuge, strength and tower. I ask You to do this great work in me. Please have Your way with my life, have Your way. Amen.

AFFIRMATION

Draw nigh to God, and he will draw nigh to you. Cleanse your hands, ye sinners; and purify your hearts, ye double minded (James 4:8).

I will draw near through my obedience.
I will draw near through my Bible studies.
I will draw near through my prayers.
I will draw near through meditating on Him.
I will draw near through trusting Him.
I will draw near through the relationships I develop.
I will draw near with the words of my mouth.
I will draw near by daily seeking His face.

These affirmations should at least help to jumpstart you in the greatest quest ever, to love Him with our ALL.

APPLICATION

Decide Today

Decisions, decisions, decisions. Many times it is very hard to determine the best decision. Someone once said "Waiting hurts. Forgetting hurts. But not knowing which decision to take can sometimes be the most painful...". Please let me assure you that a decision to pursue loving God with everything you have will not hurt or be painful. A decision to surrender all to Him and give your all to Him will lead you down a path that few get to travel.

Decide To Learn of Him

I will read (a verse, a chapter or a book). _____

_____

_____

_____

_____

I will set aside (decide on timeframe and time to read the Bible).

_____

_____

_____

Victory Scripture: Write scriptures from the word of God that you can stand on.

_____

_____

Who can you use as a resource to hold you accountable and hold you up?

_____

ABOUT THE AUTHOR

Pastor Wanda, also known as Minstrel Appointed, is the founder of Nu Mercy Christian Church in Augusta, Georgia. She is a native of Texas but has lived primarily in other states including California and Georgia. She is a college graduate who attended California State University, San Bernardino. She is an award winning Christian recording artist, publisher of the Spin Awards Magazine and Executive Producer of the Spin Awards. She also acts as an on-air radio personality. Along the way, Pastor Wanda has battled some adversity that included drug addiction, child abuse and child molestation. Her troubled years of drug addiction, child abuse and child molestation have all served to "work together for her good" as she now uses her past to help and encourage others.

CONTACT INFORMATION

Email Address: numercy@gmailcom

Website: www.appointed.mobi

SOCIAL MEDIA

Twitter: @appointend

Facebook Page: @Ministrel.Appointed

Instagram: @appointed

SELF-WORTH AND WALKING IN YOUR PURPOSE
Dior Davis

For all flesh is as grass, and all the glory of man is as the flower of grass the grass withereth, and the flower thereof falleth away. But the word of the Lord endureth forever.
1st Peter 1:24-25

I t is so amazing how the cycle of life goes and how the decisions you make can play such a vital part in your life. Even we you fall into a difficult situation and it seems like it is hard to handle, you slowly begin to see yourself falling and losing your balance and the dust begins to collect around your feet.

Trials should build patience and give you a sense of maturity. Remember, everything happens for a reason, whether or not you believe it. Even though it's hard to cope with the feeling of despair, God will always see you through.

James 1:2-3 *states "count it all joy when ye fall into divers temptations; know this that the trying of faith worketh patience."* **(KJV)**

I would like to start by sharing with you a few life changing experiences that have taken place on my journey. At a young age, I always wanted to be happily in love and married with kids. In my mind, I had to make it happen the way I wanted to have it happen. Growing up as a pastor's daughter and being the younger of two brothers, I always had this thing about proving myself to others and going about it all the wrong way. I would always dream big and always wanted to do bigger and better . Being brought up in church and having both parents in my life, one would have thought that I would have been rooted and grounded and not gullible, not falling for temptations. My parents taught me well; however, I chose a different route. Even though I would dance, put on programs, play the drums, and sing, I always felt there was a void in my life. I was lonely or needed someone in my life to make me complete not, knowing or fully understanding that loneliness is just a season and no one could make me complete. My mother would share with me, "Whoever God has for you will find you. And, as a lady, you don't look for a man. You must have integrity, standards, and don't fall for anyone and anything that someone tells you about. Never be anxious for nothing."

I was so caught up in the routine of going to church and fulfilling my obligations that I forgot about the true reason of everything I was doing. I lost sight of my relationship with GOD. I started to look in other places and at other people to fill my void.

So, I started working a good job and was doing well, furthering my career and education. All of a sudden, this guy appeared at my job *(Not knowing I was getting ready to enter into a cycle of life that I would have never thought would come my way)*.

The guy would come by my job, smile at me and tell me how beautiful I was. He would treat me to lunch and would woe me with different things every day. He told me if I would give him a chance, he could prove to me that we would be perfect together.

(Satan hears your thoughts and wants just like God)

STEP INTO THE PIVOTAL POINT IN YOUR LIFE HAVING NO FEAR AND NO REGRETS.

At work, all I could think about was having someone I might want to give a try. So, me and my new guy went to lunch, I told him I would date him. We exchanged numbers, and I began to share with him that I was a pastor's daughter, and I was in graduate school. I told him the college I attended, things I liked to do, places I wanted to go. Basically, I gave him my whole bio in one hour. After I finished, we hugged and went back to work. I learned nothing about him because I was too busy giving him all my information and glad he was giving me all his attention.

As we got deeper involved, this guy begin to beat me and hit me in places people couldn't see being that I worked in a well-known job and was in the spotlight, always performing. Every day, he would say I was nothing. I needed to survive. Even though I fought back, I had to understand that you can't fight satan in the natural, you will lose every time.

26

One day, I was at my last lab on a Saturday, and I began to get an uneasy feeling in my stomach. (Take heed to warnings the Lord gives you). He showed up wanting to argue. As I walked away, he started to grab me and I rushed to get into the car as he jumped inside, still arguing. The next thing I knew he hit me and started pounding so hard I thought I was going to die. I was screaming for help, and it seemed like my life was flashing before me. All I could do was call on the name of the Lord to save me from this horrible situation. As soon as I began to call on the Lord, the guy fled, and I was taken to the hospital.

INDULGE IN LIFE WITH GOODNESS AND NEVER GIVE UP.

At the same time, he told me he loved me. He told he had my back; he said we would never fight again, even though I would fight him weekly. It was evident from the abuse I received that he truly did not love me. He was just filling a void of being lonely. His words were empty promises. I wanted to leave him, but I remained for the wrong reasons. The longer I stayed the more I hurt myself. I stayed because I didn't want to feel embarrassed being that I was a well-known poet, had a youth outreach ministry and worked at a TV station. Again, I stayed because I didn't want to bring shame to my father and his ministry. I remained because it was easier to keep the drama between us until the last hit. God said, "Enough is enough."

The tongue is full of iniquity and can be deadly, and sometimes our own heart deceives us. When that happens, we then are affected with STDS-STINKING THINKING DISORDERS (In the words of Keith Preacher Brown). I thought that my image was more important than my own self-worth. I shut God out, and I was more hurt, abused mentally, and stressed out because what I thought was real turned out to false.

You may or may not be going through this same situation, but you may be feeling lonely, unloved or a need to be loved. Well, once you get that vision of GOD and begin to have that relationship, he will love you more than anything. You are his chosen one. Having a form of religion is not having a relationship with God.

Did you know, in order for you to be in love, you have to love God first and self-second? Then, you can love others. In order to get your breakthrough, you have to tell the Lord you are an open vessel, ready to be used by him. When you have gotten to the point in your life that you are able to sit still and listen and not be boastful when someone is giving you sound advice, that's when you know you are humble.

In Matthew 8:13, it says, "We have been crowned with Glory and Honor." Therefore, Inhale and Exhale; this is just a season. Now, are you going to stand there and let your feet collect dust because you are becoming content in this temporary position? NO, GET UP AND RENEW YOUR MIND.

Submit and humble yourself unto the Lord. Understand that God can bring peace to your mind, even at your moment of despair, he can heal your broken heart.

I learned that I had to experience something in order to believe, and I couldn't believe until I saw my worth. When that happens, it goes pass your mind into your soul, and you can begin to speak from your spirit.

DON'T GET COMPLACENT, IT'S A BEAUTIFUL DAY.

It is impossible to fight satan and his tactics in the natural.

As you take God's promises and stand on his word, say this below:

This is God's word. To know it, I must read it to understand it. I must study and to be blessed. I must live it. I am what his word says I am, and I can do what his word said I can do.

My praise is what gets God's attention, and my worship ushers him in so I can walk in my deliverance and feel God's love. When my trials come, just " Inhale and Exhale because this is just a season so take a stand and walk in Peace."

SUPPLICATION

Dear Heavenly Father,

I thank you in advance for keeping me, restoring me, and giving me strength to sustain my many trials of oppression. Yeshua, I continue to seek you daily for direction and come before your throne humbly as I know how. In your word, you said you would fight all my battles and that I needed to lay them at the altar. Now, satan, I denounce your name and all tricks that try to attack my mind, my body, my family, my business and my visions. I declare right now in your name, Yeshua, that the enemy is defeated as I take a stand and tear down the walls opposition. I am more than a conquer in Christ. You are Jehovah Rapha and my Prince of Peace. I will love you forever I offer this prayer in your name Yeshua, Amen.

AFFIRMATION:

This is God's word. To know it, I must read it.

To understand it, I must study it.

To be blessed, I must live it.

I am what his word says I am.

I can do what his word says I can do.

My praise is what gets God's attention.

My worship ushers him in so I can walk into my deliverance and feel God's love.

APPLICATION:

Take A Stand

Life can be a vicious cycle of pain despair, hurt, setbacks and distractions. When I begin to let go and let God carve my pathways, I am BOLD as a Lion and cannot be moved. I have the courage and strength to win any battle with the help of God.

Take a Stand Proclamation

I'm taking a stand against all negativity and all negative people who do not have the vision of God.

To overcome my challenges, I will step back, inhale, and exhale. I start a self-examination so I can shift my paradigm to stay in tune with the word of God and walk in peace.

Victory Scripture:

James 1:2-3 states, "Count it all joy when ye fall into divers of temptations; know this that the trying of faith worketh patience (KJV)."

Psalms 119:105 "Thy word is a lamp unto my feet and a light unto my path (KJV)."

Who can you use as a resource to hold you accountable and hold you up?

ABOUT THE AUTHOR

Dior Davis

Co-Founder & President of Truth Honey Corporation & Founder of Truth Honey Wellness.

Dior Davis is a Motivational/ Empowerment Speaker for Corporate Businesses and the Community for Entrepreneurship. After starting Truth Honey, Dior realized there was a need in the community to empower individuals and the youth to be healthy mentally, physically, spiritually and how to obtain entrepreneurship and sustainability. Truth Honey is a new line of Pure, Natural and An Elegant Brand of Honey. The company was created due to the lack of honey variety, Black Beekeepers, and the knowledge of Agriculture in our Communities.

Dior Davis and her brother started a non-profit program called "Save The Honey Bees." This non-profit program entails going into all the South Fulton Schools, teaching students, teachers and parents about the benefits of Bees and Agriculture and getting the school STEM/STEAM certified.

Dior Davis has created a Rejuvenate Wellness Drink since her near death experience where she went off an embankment, flew into a tree and is still standing. This drink has aided in healing inflammation, headaches, muscle cramps, giving a person energy, and the ability to rejuvenate their life just as Dior did.

Being a former first lady, Dior's passion has always been about uplifting women through poetry and motivational speaking. Dior's expertise is helping women understand their Self-Worth, recognizing their truth and fulfilling their purpose.

CONTACT INFORMATION

Email Address: dior.truthhoney7@gmail.com

Website: www.truthhoney.com

SOCIAL MEDIA

Facebook Page: Truth Honey Dior

Instagram: @thepageoftruthhoney

ALL THINGS NEW

Sharon Jones

" Jesus said unto him, Thou shalt love the Lord, they
God with all thy soul, and with all thy mind; This is
the first and great commandment; And the second is
like unto it, Thou shalt love thy neighbor as thyself.
Matthew 22:37-39 (KJV)

As a Christian believer, the foundation of any good relationship begins with a sound relationship with God, the heavenly Father.

Love is the key and core to a good relationship. The scriptures remind us in Matthew 22:37-39 (KJV), "Jesus said unto him, thou shalt love the Lord thy God with all thy soul, and with all thy mind; this is the first and great commandment; and the second is like unto it, thou shalt love thy neighbor as thyself."

Unfortunately, our (relationship) is at the level that we actually love ourselves.

How can you not love God? God is love. God is faithful. God is our protector, provider and our friend. God never fails; He has never left us or forsaken us. Proverbs 18:24 reminds us of the following, "A man that has friends must shew himself friendly: and there…..is a friend that sticketh closer than a brother."

Let me share my beginning. I was born in Brooklyn. I am the oldest of 3 children born to my parents; they have no other children. My parents married young and were 21 years old at the time of my birth. My father witnessed the murder of his own father as a child and was raised (with his siblings) by his mother. My mother was raised by both parents in a home where love was not expressed.

Our family eventually moved to Queens. As a child, I would witness physical abuse that my father inflicted on my mother. My parents separated and would finally divorce a few years later by the time I was around 8 years old. My mother went from a stay at home/working occasional mom to a working mom. Mommy worked while we were in school and our sister went to the local head start. We would let ourselves in the house and locked the door until she came home from work after she picked up our baby sister.

The way I felt about my self-started taking shape when I was sexually molested by one of the sons of the babysitter. I was not in school yet, so I had to be about 4 or 5 years old. I was forced not to tell. He would take me to the bedroom he shared with another brother. The perpetrator would put his finger to his lips. "Shhhhhh," he would say. "Don't tell anyone."

This would happen repeatedly while at the babysitter house. The antics would occur when his mother would leave the house to run errands. One other incident I remember was being burned when someone sat me on the hot radiator, and I was burned on my bottom. The burn was so bad I couldn't sit down without hurting. Mom abruptly stopped sending us to the babysitter after this incident.

While growing up, I would be teased by the kids in the neighborhood. My body developed "early," and I would get teased about that. I would also get teased about my looks and be called ugly. My skin is dark. I had developed acne and had course hair that my mom would keep braided until time to take school pictures. My parents also had divorced by that time, so we were not buying clothes as much and would repeat and mix and match them. Someone was always making fun of me for any of those reasons. Being teased contributed to how I saw myself and thus caused me to not love or like myself. I was insecure and also suffered with low self-esteem. I was already very shy and withdrawn. All of this happened before I finished Junior high school. I even remember overhearing a boy saying to another boy, "Her body is the only thing she has going for her." I had some friends at school and a few friends in the neighborhood. I would go outside and socialize with my neighborhood friends, but I felt more like a loner because after being around people too long, I felt that they would start to dislike me or would eventually start to tease me. I kept a barrier as a safety precaution subconsciously to avoid further hurt.

These experiences, unfortunately, shaped how I would relate and deal with other people, especially in dating relationships. In most relationships, there was insecurity on my part because I always wondered the motive of others. Many of those I met did not have agendas; unfortunately, others did. When the motives were exposed, this further piled on the insecurities. I exercised caution in building new friendships.

Our family moved again to a Queens suburb. I would miss my friends, but I was also excited as this would be a new beginning for me because I was starting high school.

In high school, I felt my life had changed. I had a social life. I was active in different clubs and organizations. I had a little more freedom to participate in many extra-curricular activities. I met many people who I am still connected to on social media today. I was on the booster squad (some schools called the booster squad the pep rally). I was a cheerleader, served in student government, secretary to the teachers, yearbook committee and several choirs. Even though I had all of these outlets, deep down, buried inside of me were the same insecurities and inadequacies.

I felt like I was in a secret sin and if I stayed around others too long, someone would figure it out and tell everyone......That is how the enemy was working in my mind.

My home life was stable. My mom worked and kept a roof over our heads. All of our needs were met. Mom told us and showed us that she loved us often.

One of my classmates invited me to join the booster squad. I tried out and I made it. The next year I was assigned to the school chorus.

The life changing event for me was joining the neighborhood community choir. A friend of mine on the booster squad invited me to come out for the choir rehearsal. It was every Saturday at 3:00 pm at a local church in the community. I joined the choir in the 10th grade and sang with them until I graduated from high school. I really enjoyed singing in the choir so much that I tried out and made it in the school gospel choir. Throughout that time, I would sing in different ensembles and the community choir sang throughout the city. The community choir was invited to do a concert in Massachusetts. I had no idea what was being set up. Throughout my life, especially as I entered adulthood, I would still sing these songs. The songs were a great set up to accept Jesus as my Lord and Savior. Many years later (July of 1991) after a devastating encounter, I rededicated my life to Jesus and decided I would learn as much about Him as I could.

I soon found out how much God loves me.

The Bible verse John 3:16 (KJV) showed me, "For God so loved the world, that he gave his only begotten Son, that whosoever believeth in him should not perish, but have everlasting life."

Another Bible verse in the book of Deuteronomy 31:6 (NIV)told me, "Be strong and courageous. Do not be afraid or terrified because of them, for the Lord your God goes with you; he will never leave you nor forsake you."

As I reflect on my past, I realize these verses to be true. There are so many reminders of God's love for me, not only in the Bible, but through experiences.

God cares for us. God cares for me; he loves me. I am the apple of God's eye.

I've learned what faith is and realize, through faith, I can do all things through Christ, who gives me strength (Phil 4:13).

I've also come to realize I cannot quit at this point in my life because God has started this process. I cannot afford to quit because I may be seconds away from my miracle. I am not angry, and my abusers are forgiven. I also forgive myself because as a child I thought that I was at fault. The abusers did not ask me to forgive them. I chose to forgive in order to heal and move forward.

Through many experiences, trials and storms in life, I am reminded that I am here for a purpose. In realizing purpose, I am intentional about understanding the purpose of the relationship with those I encounter. I don't over think the connection, but I do inquire in prayer and seek to discern. I am continually learning to love myself and understand my purpose.

Fast forward....

Note to self... In the process of living, I learned outward beauty is not where our worth lies. Proverbs 31:30 reminds us, "Charm is deceptive, and beauty is fleeting; but a woman who fears the Lord is to be praised."

Jeremiah 1:5 (KJV) reminds me, "Before I formed thee in the belly I knew thee, and before thou camest out of the womb, I sanctified thee, and I ordained thee a prophet unto the nations."

With all glory and honor to God, I know that I am an original creation..... Psalm 139:14 (KJV)reminds me, "I will praise thee; for I am fearfully and wonderfully made; marvelous are thy works; and that my soul knoweth right well.

God always provides a fresh start. Revelations 21:5 (KJV) reminds me that "And he that sat upon the throne said, Behold, I make all things new. And he said unto me, Write: for these words are true and faithful."

SUPPLICATION:

Dear heavenly Father, I praise you, glorify and magnify your name. I bless your holy name.

I am thankful today, thankful for another opportunity to see a new day. I am grateful for the ability to breathe, use my limbs, see the beautiful sky. Thank you for a sound mind today.

I thank you, God, for your love for me. Help me to see myself the way you see me. Help me to love my neighbor as I love myself. Help me to love my enemies.

Thank you, God, for giving me your wisdom in all situations and decisions. Thank you for keeping your hedge of protection around me.

Forgive me for my sins, trespasses and shortcomings. Strengthen me to forgive others for the same.

Thank You for your love, peace and protection, in your mighty name I pray,

Amen.

AFFIRMATION:

Isaiah 43:2, "When you go through deep waters, I will be with you. When you go through rivers of difficulty, you will not drown. When you walk through the fire of oppression, you will not be burned up; the flames will not consume you...."

1 John 1:9, "If we confess our sins, he is faithful and just and will forgive our sins and purify us from all unrighteousness."

APPLICATION:

Who needs your forgiveness? Whether they ask or not….. Whether or not you think they deserve forgiveness……

_____

_____

_____

_____

_____

_____

What are you forgiving them for? Say it, say it loud, write it….. You must deal with this..

1. Every day, I choose the positive. How can you look at any situation differently?

2. Think about something that really makes you smile. Write it down and discuss why this makes you smile.

Do this daily in a journal format (if you don't have a journal, you can use a notebook). This will only take a few minutes.

_____

_____

_____

_____

_____

_____

_____

_____

_____

_____

_____

_____

_____

_____

_____

_____

_____

_____

_____

ABOUT THE AUTHOR

Lady Sharon Jones is the CEO of Queendominion Enterprise, LLC (established 2011) and Executive Director and Founder of Women on the Front Line Global Outreach Ministries (established November 2013) where the vision is Transforming Lives, Impacting Generations. WOTFL Mission is To encourage, empower and support women of current and future generations to live a victorious life in Christ according to Bible scripture 3 John 2 "Beloved, I wish above all things that thou mayest prosper and be in health, even as thy soul prospereth." Lady Sharon is a New York native who has made Atlanta her home.

Lady Sharon has earned a Bachelor's Degree from Queens College (Flushing, NY), Master of Science Degree (Public Administration Concentration) from Central Michigan University and a Graduate Certificate in Project Management from Capella University.

Lady Sharon has also received certificates of completion for "When Leaders Lead" taught by the late Bishop Earl Paulk from the Cathedral of the Holy Spirit and Master Life Discipleship Series.

Lady Sharon served in the U.S. Army Reserves over 20 years and completed service at the Officer rank of Captain. She currently serves as a board member with Pillar of Fire Christian Ministries, Biloxi, MS, Pathway Christian Ministries, in Atlanta GA and formerly with The Elect Lady Ministries, McDonough, GA.

When not working or serving in ministry, Sharon enjoys reading and spending time with family. Lady Sharon, the wife, mother, sister, daughter and friend aspires to live her life according to God's promise in 3 John 2.

CONTACT INFORMATION
Email Address: wotflglobal@gmail.com

Website:

SOCIAL MEDIA

Facebook Page: @wotflglobal

Instagram: @wotflglobal

WHAT ARE YOU WEARING TONIGHT?
Nicky Bruyning

She girds herself with strength, and strengthens her arms.
Strength and honor are her clothing; she shall rejoice in time to come
Proverbs 31:17 & 25

I had it all - all the love a girl could ask for from both parents, a Christian upbringing, first class education, great friendships, awards, trophies and a comfortable, happy life growing up in the tiny country of Guyana, South America. There I was – a bold immigrant girl in a new world in the USA, off to a running start at one of the best universities in the state of Maryland. My goals were clear: education first, then marriage, a family and somewhere along that timeline earn a Doctorate degree in Psychology.

It all came to a screeching halt when I found out I was pregnant in my second semester of college. My life would never be the same. This was the beginning of my testing ground; the beginning of when and how I proved that the strength within me prevails. The next eight years of my life would be riddled with deep, dark valleys of trial and testing. During my "happy" years as a teenager I had always clung to the scripture "Yet in these things we are more than conquerors through him who loved us" (Romans 8:37). And even as I clung to it, I always thought to myself that in order to be a conqueror, there must be a battle to fight, a war to wage and a victory to claim. Life had been easy - until then..

My boyfriend (and later husband, now ex-husband) and father of my children loved me dearly - so he thought, and so I believed. What did this so-called love look like? Infidelity; emotional and verbal hammering on my psyche; the very same lips that kissed me hurled words that eroded and diminished my self-worth and cut to the core of my being; the same hands that caressed my body, held me and made me feel safe, registered striking blows to my head, belly, arms, thighs, and all parts of my body leaving me bruised, aching and broken in ways I try to forget.

Quote:

Just like a seed hides itself away in the dirt, and a caterpillar hides in its cocoon, the strength of who you truly are germinates in the unseen.

I was tested to the point of a suicide attempt - in that moment I had preferred to be absent from my painful, torturous existence with this man, than to endure another waking moment. My focus was consumed with the noise and the darkness. I had lost sight of who I was - although who I was had NOTHING to do with this man and what he chose to drag me through. I had lost sight of the power of love - love itself, love for me, love for my babies, love for life. And rather than clothing myself in the strength that was waiting right there inside of me, waiting to be unleashed, I chose to cower and escape it all. As I swallowed the last pill and sat there feeling myself slip away, the God in me reminded me that my work as mother was not yet finished, that my children needed me. This was my rescue. This was the beginning of my awakening.

Strength comes through testing. How do you know you're strong until you've performed a task that requires strength? It took life breaking me for me to produce the evidence of who I was at my core - strong and honorable. Does this mean that I was perfect or blemish-free? Absolutely not. It means that despite my imperfections what God deposited in me from the beginning of time was always there. His strength was made perfect in all of my weaknesses.

Do not fall prey to the lies. There is NO FEAR in love. There is only POWER.

More often than not, it is when a woman comes to the end of herself, being tested to her very core, that she finds her strength; her true, divine strength that existed from the very inception; her immense love and light, the very essence of her being. Proverbs 31:17 & 25 documents the extraordinary worth of a virtuous woman who girds (secures or equips) herself with strength and clothes (adorns or covers) herself in strength and honor. Being "girded" strongly suggests that the virtuous woman is in a state of readiness, armed with strength for that time of reckoning.

What's *your* stance?

She embodies security, stability and power. During the time period of the old testament an individual's garment strongly signified who he/she was in society. One's robe or coat could have very well served to identify social status. For example, the king's virgin daughters wore special robes that served as evidence of a position of honor. The Proverbs 31 woman's "robe" is her strength and honor - this is her covering, the evidence of who she is. She is an immovable woman of integrity whose worth brings high esteem to the office of womanhood itself.

What serves as *your* evidence? What are you wearing that signifies who you are?

The Proverbs 31 woman has found her place in her Creator, and though her physical strength may fade with age, she still remains a woman of inherent strength and honor. There is a resilience that causes her to keep going when EVERYTHING in her path says STOP. When those around her cry out for help - she reaches within, knowing her source is Divine, and extends her hand to bestow healing.

We must embrace the disruption that comes into our lives. In the midst of the disruption, hardship and pain come the beauty, strength and resilience.

You are her. You are that woman of strength and honor, masterfully fashioned by the Master Creator himself. Within you, oh woman of this time, is an untapped strength that will cause the forward movement of nations - they will no longer be stagnant, but will flourish as you flourish. With your strong outstretched arm you will meet the needs of the poor and give life to the dying.

Your strength and honor will go before you causing lasting transformation. It is a strength that endures; a strength that incubates seed and brings forth life; a strength that brings healing and enables you to absorb the mess and turmoil and restore order - within yourself and in others.

You are the answer to many questions, and the solution to problems unimaginable. There is a quiet stillness in your soul that possesses immeasurable strength, a strength found when you lose yourself in the presence of the One who fashioned you.

In your breaking, may you come to the knowledge of true love, to the knowledge of your true eternal self; embracing, loving, caressing *all* of your divine feminineness - this is where your strength lies. As you fall in love with the unadulterated essence of **your** womanhood this is when you find your voice.

So, now, gird yourself, equip yourself, ready yourself- for you will be tested. And when that day comes, may you be found royally clothed in strength and honor.

And may you rejoice in time... it's on its way!

SUPPLICATION

Oh, Mighty Creator of the universe and my soul, I am grateful for your peace, your joy unspeakable, and your steadfast love. I believe that it is in You I live and move and have my being. I ask that you illuminate my soul with your glorious light. Captivate my mind with the fullness of your marvelous creation in me, and open my eyes to the radiant strength of who I am as *woman*. Amen.

AFFIRMATION

I am light; I am love.

I am the sweet, melodious expression of God.

I am clothed in strength and covered in honor.

For any test, I am ready.

For any battle, I have already won the victory.

Every experience past, present & future is subject to my authority.

I am powerful; I am strong.

APPLICATION

From this day forth, the choice is yours; how you view yourself, treat yourself and conduct yourself is in the power of your own mind. Each day from the moment you awake to the time you close your eyes at night you have the choice and the power to take dominion over your mind.

Everyday remind yourself of *who* you are. Realize that you are an exceptional work of art. You are a woman possessing divine virtues - it is up to you to simply decide to live and walk in this identity, this sense of self. Therefore, re-claim yourself, live in the power of this knowingness. Knowing that even if you are unable to conceive a child, or your marriage didn't last, or you are still wounded from past relationships or experiences - your radiance, your true feminine essence still remains. Harness this power and bring all of the mess under subjugation. What's been done *to* you does not define you. Your current circumstance is simply that - circumstance - it is not *you*. Go within yourself with the confidence that you have so much to give. You are an incubator of seed - spiritual and/or physical - with the miraculous ability to nurture that seed and birth life. The answers, the strength, each day, are within...

ABOUT THE AUTHOR

Nicky Bruyning, Founder & CEO
Dawn Your Confidence, LLC

Radio personality, Motivational Speaker and Founder & CEO of Dawn Your Confidence, LLC (DYC), Nicky Bruyning's life is filled with work that allows her to be of service to others. It is no coincidence that she has chosen this path. It is her life's mission to help women, who she considers to be nurturers of life, to pursue more confident and fulfilling lives. It is to this end that Nicky created DYC. Through DYC Nicky hosts annual retreats, seminars and weekly connections on social media for women, with the goal of providing a nurturing, supportive environment for women to be rejuvenated, healed and reawakened to their greatness within.

After becoming a mother at the tender age of 19, Nicky endured years in a tumultuous relationship that tested the very fiber of her being. Refined in the fire, she has harnessed every challenge and triumph and channeled that energy for her personal growth and success. When she is not actively working on Dawn Your Confidence initiatives, speaking at special events or volunteering her time for a worthy cause, Nicky enjoys savoring the joys of motherhood, and continues to give of herself as a dedicated Registered Nurse.

Nicky Bruyning, the Uplifter of Lives, creates moments for women to authentically reconnect with their true, divine essence, while facilitating transformational connections with other feminine souls. As Nicky puts it: DYC exists as a catalyst for women to be empowered to live with vibrance, grace, beauty, strength, boldness and confidence.

CONTACT INFORMATION

Email Address: NickyB@DawnYourConfidence.com

Website: www.dawnyourconfidence.com

SOCIAL MEDIA

Twitter: @confidencedawn

Facebook Page: Dawn Your Confidence

Instagram: @dawnyourconfidence

SHOOT FOR THE STARS
Dr. Rolanda S. Watson

To whom God was pleased to make known what is the riches of the glory of this mystery among the Gentiles, which is Christ in you, the hope of glory. —
Colossians 1:27.

An exhortation to Lemuel, a young prince at the time, Proverbs 31 was given as a prophecy under the inspiration and direction of God, urging him to take heed of the sins he would be tempted with and to the duties of the place he was called. Lemuel was encouraged to search for a wife who was virtuous and capable of building and maintaining a successful home. Additionally, Lemuel was instructed to find a woman of magnificent character whose worth cannot be measured in terms of costly jewels but in measures pertaining to riches of the glory of God!

The opening words, "who can find" positions this woman as the ideal woman to choose as well as to be. The phrase virtuous woman speaks of excellence, moral worth, ability and nobility. Such a woman is the epitome of wisdom; she was an entrepreneur and a leader among women.

The woman depicted in Proverbs 31 was no ordinary woman, she was extraordinary in every possible regard. Subsequently, the way she conducted herself in her home and the work she did in her community changed the game for the nations. She was a disruptor of the status quo and established new standards that women today, can model.

The Proverbs 31 woman is the same woman personified in Ephesians 5: 25-27. She is a carrier of God's anointing, honor and glory! She is the one that Jesus is coming back to present unto Himself. This woman is the bride of Christ, the glorious church. God is not coming back for a weak pusillanimous church. Afterall, Christ is the most glorious bridegroom there ever was, and he is coming back for a bride that is sweeping in great glory, majesty and power. This woman walked in the manifest presence of God! The word of God teaches in 2 Corinthians 3: 14, "But we all, with unveiled face, beholding as in a mirror the glory of the Lord, are being transformed into the same image from glory to glory, just as by the Spirit of the Lord." In other words, as the church continues in God, we are being washed, cleansed and transformed into the same image and likeness of God from one stage of glory to another until we all reach that mature man in Christ. Moreover, this woman was multi-faceted and exemplified the multi-dimensional characteristics of God. There is an order of God in the Spirit. For example: Father, Son Holy Spirit: God is Father in creation; Son in redemption and Holy Spirit in regeneration in the saints. Another example of this would be: Jesus is the way, truth and the life…It is in Him that we live, move and have our being. More specifically, there are three dimensions of God's glory in the heavenlies. The Bible confirms this in 1 Corinthians 15: 39-41. It reads, All flesh is not the same flesh: but there is one kind of flesh of men, another flesh of beasts, another of fishes, and another of birds. There are also celestial bodies, and terrestrial bodies: but the glory of the celestial is one, and the glory of the terrestrial is another.

There is one glory of the sun, and another glory of the moon, and another glory of the stars: for one star differs from another star in glory. The apostle Paul reiterates in 2 Corinthian 12: 2, "I know a man in Christ who was caught up to the third heaven fourteen years ago. Whether he was in the body or out of the body, I don't know; God knows." In essence, the first dimension of heaven is where the birds fly in the sky. The second dimension of heaven is where the sun, moon and stars exist, and the third dimension is where God dwells. The third dimension is where God is trying to move forward, the church. This is the place where God is in complete control, a place of maturity and responsibility. A place where we stop just attending church and come to the revelation that we are the church. Taking responsibility for who we are and what we do is maturity. God is trying to get the church to a place where we are able to respond and not have someone else propel and make us ready before we can respond. When we are mature in Christ, we can worship God in Spirit and in Truth. God is moving the church forth to a place where He is able to reproduce His glory or manifest presence in the earth. When this happens, we, the church, then become carriers of His glory. When the church becomes glory carriers, we also have the ability to pass it

48

on to the next generation. There's a third woman in the Bible who demonstrates the same level of maturity revealed in Proverbs 31 and Ephesians 5: 25-27. She's found in Revelations 12: 1-2, the scripture reads as follows: "And there appeared a great wonder in heaven; a woman clothed with the sun, and the moon under her feet, and upon her head a crown of twelve stars: And she, being with child cried, travailing in birth, and pained to be delivered. While theologians would argue that this woman is natural Israel; I, however, would contend by divine revelation that this woman is the

Philippians 2:5 says, "Let this mind be in you, which was also in Christ Jesus." (KJV)

church matured to the third dimension of the glory of God. To begin with, this woman is clothed with sun. In Malachi 4: 2, the Bible teaches, But unto you that fear my name shall the Sun of righteousness arise with healing in his wings; and ye shall go forth, and grow up as calves of the stall. This woman being clothed with the sun of righteousness suggests that she is a righteous saved woman. She is wrapped in the Sun of righteousness. She has put on the Lord Jesus Christ that she would

not make provisions for the flesh, Romans 13:14. She is the righteousness of God in Christ Jesus. She has come to the realization that there is no more playing church. She is saved for real! Secondly, this woman has the moon under her feet.

The moon is a type of that which reflects the sun. The moon doesn't produce its own light. The light of the moon is a reflection of the sun. Apart from the sun, there isn't moon light. The same light that is in the sun is also in the moon; therefore, let this mind be in you, which also in Christ Jesus. The moon is symbolic of the mind or soulish nature. The soul / mind is comprised of the will, intellect and emotions; this woman is standing on top of her mind. She has her will, intellect and emotions under control. Anytime the church can stand on something, this means we have complete control and dominion over it. This woman has mastered her soulish nature and has surrendered her will to the absolute will of God. In addition to surrendering her will, she's intelligent and recognizes that she doesn't know everything and therefore, she able to sit at the feet of Jesus and be taught the word of God. This woman is humble and has a meek spirit; meaning, she has a teachable disposition. She has the ability to learn from others. She's not jealous or intimidated by other women. She knows who she is in Christ! Finally, with regard to the soulish nature, this woman has dealt with her emotions. In doing so, she will never display episodes of popping off, being disrespectful or losing control, publicly or in private. Anxiety and depression are issues of the past for this woman. Not only does she walk in the Spirit; she has also mastered the fruit of the Spirit.

Revelations 12: 1-2 also mentions that this woman has a crown of 12 stars on her head. In Isaiah 60: 1-5, the Bible reads, "Arise, shine, for your light has come, and the glory of the LORD has risen upon you. For behold, darkness shall cover the earth, and thick darkness the peoples; but the LORD will arise upon you, and his glory will be seen upon you. And nations shall come to your light, and kings to the brightness of your rising. Lift up your eyes all around, and see; they all gather together, they come to you; your sons shall come from afar, and your daughters shall be carried on the hip. Then you shall see and be radiant; your heart shall thrill and exult, because the abundance of the sea shall be turned to you, the wealth of the nations shall come to you." Once the crown of 12 stars is placed on the head of this mature wise woman by God, the nations will see her light and she will then lead the mass to Christ. Daniel 12.3 confirms this, "Those who are wise will shine like the brightness of the heavens, and those who lead many to righteousness, will shine like the stars forever and ever."

Like the Proverbs 31 woman and the woman studied in Revelations 12, it has been determined that it's not enough to be saved. This is merely the first dimension. We must move into the second dimension of God's glory whereby we are able to sit at Jesus' feet and be taught sound doctrine. Though imperative, we can't stop here. We must enter a dimension in God where we become the teacher and rivers of living water flows from our bellies. When the church has been redeemed from the hand of the enemy, God has given the authority, power and expectation to say so! We must shoot for the stars, that crown of God's glory! The woman in Revelations 12 was with child and ready to give birth which denotes she was in her third trimesters signifying her maturation and capacity to stand and reproduce in the earth after His own kind and to walk in the light of His Shekinah Glory and her prophetic destiny.

We are the glorious church that Jesus is coming back for! That church without spot or wrinkle or any such thing but, that she should be holy and without blemish.

SUPPLICATION

Dear Heavenly Father, I bless and thank you for another opportunity to enter your manifest presence of shekinah glory. Lord, it is an honor and privilege to stand before you in thanksgiving, praise and worship. Father, I understand that you are the author and finisher of my faith and it is because of you Jesus, that I have been saved by grace through faith. Thank you for loving and caring for me as you do and teaching me your Word and likeness through your precious Holy Spirit. Thank you for unveiling my eyes and making known the glorious riches and mystery of the church which is, Christ in me, the hope of Glory! Thank you for living in me and allowing your glory to shine upon my face that I can be a witness for Jesus everywhere I go. Lord, thank you for healing, delivering and setting me free. I thank you for your gifts of wisdom and knowledge that the nations will see the light of your glory and yield to the bleeding side of Calvary's cross. Lastly, Father, I thank you for your plan and third dimensional process of justification, sanctification and glorification. I thank you, Master, that I have been rescued from the penalty, power and very presence of sin. In the beautiful and loving name of the Lord Jesus Christ; the Son of the Living God I pray, Amen!

AFFIRMATION

Today, I have been enlightened by the incorruptible, indestructible seed of the living word of God.

I am a woman of God; Empowered by the Spirit of God.

I decree and declare that I am that virtuous woman portrayed in Proverbs 31.

I am that glorious church who is being washed, cleansed and in preparation for my glorious bridegroom.

I am the bride of Christ!

I am clothed in righteousness

I have my soulish nature under my feet

Above all, I have been crowned by God with an undeniable garland of 12 stars on my head, representing the glory of God!

I am saved; I have been taught and I have now become, the teacher!

I am that third dimensional woman! In Jesus' Name, Amen!

APPLICATION

Justification is the divine act of declaring sinners to be righteous on account of their faith in Christ. Sanctification is the process in which God develops the new life of the believer and gradually brings it to perfection. Glorification is the ultimate salvation of the whole person. This occurs when we are face to face with our Savior in His coming Kingdom. At this time, God will completely mold us into the image of Christ. We will then be able to enjoy complete fellowship with God, singing His praises forevermore, according to (Romans 8: 29-30 and Phil. 3:21.)

With regard to the word of God, how would you define the glory of God?

_____

_____

_____

Where are you in your walk with God as it pertains to this chapter's reading?_____

_____

_____

What are some steps you can take to further develop your process of justification, sanctification and glorification?

_____

_____

_____

What was your greatest spiritual value adopted in this chapter of influence?_____

_____

_____

ABOUT THE AUTHOR

DR. ROLANDA SELINA WATSON

A native of Biloxi, Mississippi, is the proud mother of two wonderful children and grandmother of a handsome 4 year- old little boy. Dr. Rolanda currently serves as the founder and president of Pillar of Fire Ministries originally established in 2008 in Union City, GA and re-organized in 2017 in Biloxi, Mississippi. With a vision to encourage present leaders and build future leaders in business and ministry, Dr. Watson has served in several leadership positions within the Church and has a wide-range of experience in business administration and management. In addition to speaking and consulting, Dr. Watson is committed to empowering and assisting aspiring women in becoming entrepreneurs.

Dr. Watson was licensed in ministry in 2006 and ordained to the office of Prophet in 2008 under the leadership of Begin Again Ministries in Atlanta, Georgia. Rolanda holds a Bachelor of Arts in Journalism and a graduate of Aaron's Beard Bible College: School of the Prophets. Moreover, Dr. Rolanda received her Master of Business Administration (MBA) in 2011 and Post- Master's Certificate in Education with a specialization in College Teaching in 2013. Lastly, Dr. Watson, has completed a Doctor of Ministry (D. Min.) in Pastoral Leadership in 2014; She has also completed the coursework for a Doctor of Education (Ed. D) in Educational Leadership and Management. With a number of entrepreneurial ventures achieved. Dr. Watson has also served in the United States Army Quartermaster Corps specializing in Logistics, stationed at Fort Lee. Virginia.

CONTACT INFORMATION

Email Address: Watson.rolanda@icloud.com

SOCIAL MEDIA

Twitter: @mbmtravel

Facebook Page: @watson.rolanda

Instagram: @Rolandaswatson

YOUR PURPOSE, GOD'S PROMISE
Gail R. Cunningham

Everything comes from God alone. Everything lives by his power, and everything is for his glory. To him be glory evermore.
Romans 11:36

Paul declares with assurance that the universe belongs to God, and we are simply living in it and part of it. He began to build upon the question he asked in the previous verse: Who has given anything to God valuable enough that God owes him something back? The answer is nobody. So often we find ourselves in the state of mind thinking God owes us. The fact of the matter is God doesn't owe us anything. Paul did a great job explaining why everything that is in the universe came from God. He is the creator and the source of all that is good, and he is the ruler over every living and dead thing.

This means, not only is God the source of all things, He holds them together and directs them how he so pleases. He sustains everything and aligns things that are to come. All things that exist continues through Him, all things are to Him or for Him. In other words, everything that exists has been made for God's purposes. It all reflects glory back to him. There is nothing that exists that hasn't been made for God's purpose. Paul concludes with a statement of great worship: To God be glory forever. It's both a statement of fact and prayer for its fulfillment. He ends this letter by saying "Amen"…meaning, so be it and let it be so. Growing up with a single mom who successfully raised 11 children on her own. I must admit, despite how strong and well-groomed we were as a family, we all had our challenges. There were times when peace in our home was far in between. I was constantly being told I look just like my father and would not amount to anything other than to have a multitude of children. I drowned myself in secular music and from time to time wrote lyrics to wrap songs as an outlet to get out my anger.

As years went on and my desire to be loved took a turn for the worst. I ran away from home and met a man that took me away from my family and abused me mentally and physically several times per day, every day. I was raped and held hostage. Countless nights, I would ask God, "What have I done to deserve this." I would try to physically escape, and the abuse got worse. I recall being dragged outside with no clothes on and then taken to the nearest bridge to throw me over it. I prayed, "God, please don't let me die." As time went on, I started losing hope. I felt my life went from one extreme to another, being pregnant and given several sexually transmitted diseases repeatedly. As if that wasn't the worst thing that could have happened to me, I found out the man who impregnated me was in love with a man whom he'd been in a relationship with for years. I remember asking God to remove this man from my life before I potentially contracted aids, and God answered my prayers, the day my daughter turned one month old.

After that, instead of turning to God, I believed I had to be hard and go out and get what no man would offer me. I began to crave the finer things in life. I turned to selling drugs, and the thought to trust no man just as my mom taught me burned deep within my soul. I was taught to never let anyone see me weak, but all along, I was hurting and weak and continued to thirst for true love and a better way. It was a day I will never forget; I met my soon to be husband, who I believed was the complete opposite of what I had experienced. He was such a gentleman and treated me with such care. He tapped into my soft side in which I thought possibly didn't exist anymore. *What a well-spoken church going man.* I would think to myself and a man who loved his mom and treated my daughter as if she was his very own. I recall him telling me, "You are too pretty to have such a dirty mouth, and I don't want you to use that type of language." Although I took that into consideration, that was all I knew… when I was angry, I expressed it and was sure to give it my best. I grew up being told to think the worst before the best and then when something unfavorable happens, you won't be surprised or hurt, not knowing that way of thinking would only hurt me.

Too my surprise, my soon to be sister in law asked me to go to church with her, and I took her up on the offer. That was a life changing moment for me. Who would have known that one single church visit would change my life forever? I felt as though the pastor was speaking directly to me. He began to talk about what we go through isn't always about us; God uses these things to press the best out of us. I wanted to hear more teachings from the speaker and had never heard the word of God broken down to where I could relate. Praise and worship service allowed me to pour out and release all the pain that was embedded for years. I had to tell everybody about the experience. My guards went from not letting anyone know the real me and being trapped in a painful box, to letting in one person at a time. I felt like I was on top of the world until I discovered my soon to be husband had a hang up that once made me think I was the only one, left me feeling like I wasn't good enough due to the constant infidelity. Instead of turning to the world,

I turned to what I knew would give me true comfort and a lasting feeling of hope and love. I began going to church, seeking God and soon got a feel for my purpose. During my quiet time, God would remind me of the times he was revealing my purpose even as a child. Showing me, "For every time you felt misunderstood and was abused, I was there carving out your purpose." I recalled the times God would speak to me as a child and my mom would ask me to sing to her, lay hands on her and pray. Immediately she would be healed. I recall hearing and speaking things and they would come to pass. I begin praying and counseling people with no experience, only to go off of what I knew to be the promises of God for his people, and change would take place.

As the years progressed, my hunger for the Lord deepened, and my faith and strength in God increased. Opposition was thrown at me to a greater magnitude. Now pregnant with my 3rd child, witchcraft was put on me with a goal to abort my baby and destroy my relationship with my husband. Even though this was a dark and devastating time in my life, what was meant for evil, God turned it around and made it work for my good. We don't always see the outcome before the beginning but God does. Had I known God would give me dominion over the spirit of witchcraft, I would have reacted just the same as Paul did… knowing that nothing can get through God unless given the right of passage. I've now learned to respond in a way that will give glory to God and defame and strip Satan of the power he thinks he has. When I was diagnosed with what would have been stage four cancer, I never spoke of what the earthly doctor said I had. Instead, I kept this between me and God. I recall telling the Lord, "It ain't so," and I trusted God in every way I knew how. He was so faithful to me to complete purpose and live to testify to all that God healed me and demonstrated his promise in my life. The doctor could not find evidence or a trace of cancer in my body. I believe none of this would have taken place in my life until I realized… What I went through was only to fulfill the purpose of healing, deliverance, restoration and forgiveness.

SUPPLICATION

I pray that God will reveal your purpose through every test and trial you've endured, and you will receive the promises of God that were assigned to you from the beginning of time.

Pray with me. Lord, I empty out everything of my past that contributes to heartache, disappointment, and unforgiveness in my life. Lord, I thank you for continuing to mold and guide me fulfilling what you have already begun. I speak that the all-consuming fire will set ablaze the deep seeded soul wounds from my past and that the healing balm of Gilead will rest upon me suddenly. What the devil meant for my evil, I thank you, Lord, for turning it around and making it for my good. Each day I am looking forward to a refreshing filled with my purpose and your promises…Lord, God, I now take on who you said I am, and I believe, understand and know, that promise is my portion today. In Jesus' name, Amen.

AFFIRMATION

For 21 days, declare these words:

My purpose was produced through my pain.

I walk in purpose and operate through promise.

My past ignites my purpose.

I'm holding on to God's Promises.

I was built for purpose to receive promise.

Nothing can get through God unless given the right of passage.

My life has promise written all over it.

I'm Purpose Driven.

APPLICATION

Throughout our purpose filled journey, often times we can't see the hand of God because situations grasp our attention. Can you think back in your life when you endured and went through the test of times and how God's hand was on your life? List supporting details associated with the difference or view you see now versus then------------------------------------

Ever wondered what is your purpose? Think about what you were going through then (past) that you find yourself ministering to and encouraging others about now? ---. Well, that's your purpose.

Recite at least 3 scriptures associated with your purpose and God's promise ---

ABOUT THE AUTHOR

Transformational Teacher, Purpose Revivalist, SOUL Shifter, Kingdom Ambassador, Gail Cunningham comes to ignite your purpose, passion, and profits. She is an intentional leader whose passion reaches to meet the needs of others. Gail thrives on providing lifelong tools that assist others in fulfilling their purpose. This revolutionary speaker is influencing and impacting lives through her out of box training that concentrates on renewing the mind, heart, and soul. Her teaching brings forth healing, restoration, and transformation in the lives that she touches. She is equipping generations to change nations.

Mrs. Cunningham is transforming lives through her entrepreneur endeavors. Her organization, Women of Influence Ink, is rewriting the narrative of many women's lives as she helps them identify their purpose and develop and execute an action plan so they may live a purposeful life. Her Lollipop Glam Boutique (is assisting others in making their mark in society by identifying their internal and external beauty). She (produces productive citizens) through her Tower Staffing Solutions. Gail is maximizing her influence and reach in radio through her shows Spring Forward.

Gail serves faithfully as the cofounder of Nations of Fire Ministry alongside her husband, Pastor Aaron Cunningham. Mrs. Cunningham is the mother of five biological children and one bonus blessing. She extends herself to those who are hurting, low income, or broken and provide them with life strategy tools to come out of their situation.

Gail Cunningham is here to influence, impact, and ignite the purpose within you.

CONTACT INFORMATION

Email Address: gail@ gailrcunningham.com

Website: www. gailrcunningham.com

SOCIAL MEDIA

Twitter:

Facebook Page: @grcunningham

Instagram: @grcunningham

LOOK AT THE SIGNS IN YOUR LIFE
Barbara Beckley

Let each of you look not only to his own interests,
but also to the interests of others
Philippians 2:4

D o you sometimes ask yourself why certain things happen in your life and what does it truly mean for you. In the Book of Philippians, Paul wrote a letter of thankfulness to the Philippians because they were very humble and generous towards his mission to be able to speak to others about the gospel. Paul explained they were a great example of not only paying attention to their own needs within their village but was willing to look beyond and support him mentally and financially. The letter was from Paul being imprisoned but was now able to do the things he wanted to do. It was very comforting to him to know he had people outside to care and believe in him in spite of the trials and events that were happening to him. It could not stop the gospel from being heard.

The Philippians showed a spirit of giving, sacrifice and being a community to show leadership on how to serve others and to help them know their purpose, not only as individuals but as a group. As Paul was imprisoned, he still had a job to do and a purpose. In addition, the Philippians had a purpose to not only support Paul but to be an example to other tribes.

We need to support and have that "interest" for others and not just for ourselves. This is where the magic happens because we are not making it about us anymore, and the blessing comes into play to take care of our needs.

I can truly relate to Paul on getting the message out to others. But I was still battling with a tug of war in my life. Now, Paul had to deal with physical and mental imprisonment, which is something that I am familiar with. It started at a very young age and held me captive for over 30 years of my life. I remember at the age of seven the children at school thinking and telling me that I was stupid, ugly, and insignificant. Their torment initiated a desire of not wanting to go to school as they thought my attendance was useless.

Right here is where I began to go into a mental prison cell as I isolated myself from others, didn't talk or express myself in any way. I just kept to myself. I was drawn to this decision because the other children did not want to hear from, me and they had pre judgmental thoughts about me. If this wasn't enough, I was being bullied for over two years from the age of 8 to 10. I didn't tell anybody because they threaten to beat me up and have someone to hurt my parents. At an early age, I had to deal with fear, judgment, and identity crisis. These were all the tools that incarcerated my mind.

I became like Paul, put behind bars, but it was not physical, it was mental. This stronghold existed because I was young and did not understand not to let others influence me to go into my shell. I didn't know how to move forward and recognize that I was special and did not need to allow their negative words to get into my head. Words are powerful, and they shape environments and lives. They are seeds that are planted within our minds that grow and produce positive or negative lifestyles. That's why it's crucial to adhere to Ephesians 4:29-30.

"Let no corrupt word proceed out of your mouth, but what is good for necessary edification, that it may impart grace to the hearers. And do not grieve the Holy Spirit of God …

Seeds from corrupt words imprisoned me in my mind as it has done others. They started me on a negative path of insecurities, isolation from others, unable to express myself, and hiding from my passion. It's so important to understand your passion and purpose because they are truly your foundation and permission to move forth in your God-ordained assignment. It will provide you with the strength you need to overcome the storms and earthquakes that show up on your path. I'm sure the Proverbs 31 Woman had many adversities, but she didn't allow them to hinder her purpose.

To live a virtuous life, we must go back and find the root of every issue that has hindered us from the work of God. We must be willing to deal with each one accordingly. In over 30 years of captivity, there were people who spoke positive words in my life, but as a child, it was difficult to believe when everything else spoke something different. However, when I was in my place of isolation, I distinctively remember three individuals that planted positive seeds that eventually begin to produce life in me. My father, who is my Rock, my 7th-grade teacher and a special nurse saved my life.

It began with my father believing in me and planting the seeds in my mind to know I was important and had a special gift. At that time, I couldn't conceive it, but I thank God that he had the wisdom to release impactful words that eventually brought me out of my mental prison. When I would come from school, feeling sad, he would always tell me "You are a very special little girl, a diamond in the rough. You are being made and polished to shine very brightly in the world." Being that I was seven, I did not understand the whole statement, but I was drawn to the word "Diamond" because I related it to pretty and shiny.

His words became rooted in my mind and started the **growing** thought that I am worth something in life.

My father would remind me every day, when I came home from school, that I was not a failure, stupid or ugly. He knew repetition was essential to continue to understand a point, to believe in a cause, and to persuade me. My Father understood the power of words and wanted to make sure I understood my identity. My mother, on the other hand, looked at words differently, she thought if she stated I was not that smart and did not look so pretty, I would work on it harder and put items into action. She did not realize it was feeding the negative words that I was receiving from my classmates and the bully on the bus that was assigned to me. I just mentioned "Bully assigned to me." At the time, this was not the thought process at all. I now understand it was a part of my development process that was molding me into the diamond my father described. Always remember, events in our lives are stepping stones to our purpose and greatness within us. Make sure you understand the signs in your life that are assisting you to the next level in your path of purpose. The words of my father were confirmed through my 7th-grade teacher as she watered the seed of a diamond within me. She was very hard on us and made sure we followed our assignment and did our homework. Out of love, she did not take excuses from us because she genuinely wanted us to be what we were designed to become.

I adored my teacher because she was attentive and aware of what was going on in her classroom. She saw the other children verbally abusing me with word that were incarcerating me in my mind. She would always pull me to the side before leaving to go home and tell me, "Barbara J. Beckley, remember you are unique and being molded, just like a diamond in the rough. Keep your head up and know I believe in you." Now I first thought, "How did she know my father was telling me this at home and are they in this together? But I found out, my father did not have a clue my teacher was speaking the same powerful words over my life. Look at the sign of how God was reinforcing His purpose for my life, again repetition. This continued to crack the door open from my prison cell and gave me more hope.

Confirmation is so important when you are working towards your purpose. It is like having someone or some events leaving "bread crumbs" on your path in life. You must have an open mind that's attentive to what is being stated and what is going on around you to make sure you do not miss those moments of clarity for your life. It started when I was younger, but one thing I continue to remember was the diamond being mentioned, and it would pull me a step closer out of the darkness. What signs and confirmation have you been receiving towards your purpose and your value? Have the positive seeds that have been planted in your life become your confirmation to move forward? It's so important to listen and beware of those signs in your life. Someone once said,

"If you hear the same things more than 3 times, maybe you need to listen and look at what is being said." It could possibly be leading you on the path to unveiling the virtuous woman within you or warn you from that which comes to steal your virtue.

My 3rd confirmation was at the age of 17; I had just received the most tragic news of my life a few days prior. It was a Thanksgiving I would never forget. My father, my rock, the person who reinforced my image according to God, had passed away. What was I going to do now that the foundation in my life was gone from my life and the person that believed in me?

The passing was not from a sickness or an accident, but my father was murdered, life was taken away. My mother got a phone call from the police and had to tell me the horrifying news. When I heard it, I completely lost it. I went to my room, slammed the door and became a tornado. I tore up my room and was not myself for 30 minutes. When the paramedics arrived, they had to knock the door down to get me out and take me to the hospital for observation, a 48 hour suicide watch.

Have you ever dealt with so much pain that it was so overwhelming? Therefore, words are so powerful. The scriptures remind us in Romans 8:28 "And we know that for those who love God all things work together for good, for those who are called according to his purpose." Again, purpose was popping up in my life. When I was in the hospital under observation, suicidal thoughts were going through my mind. I said to myself, "I might as well join Daddy since he was my encourager. How will I go on now?" I made up in my mind I was going to end it. But through God's intervention, another sign came to me that redirected me back to purpose and the revealing of the virtuous woman within me.

The nurse on duty just came into my room for a blood pressure check. As she was preparing to place the blood pressure equipment on my arm, she looked into my eyes and told me, "I truly believe your loved one that passed away would not want you to think certain thoughts you are having right now. They would want you to continue your life and move forward. Certain events happen in all our lives that continue to polish and mold us just like the diamond in the rough, to become an amazing gem that will shine bright and help others."

At that moment, something profound happened that unified my mind, spirit, and soul as one, with the truth that set me free. It confirmed and let me know how important it was to continue my life. The nurse did not know my father, my 7th grade school teacher, and all of them stated that I was a diamond in the rough. Now, you know I had to follow the signs that were unlocking the virtuous woman within. This is an excellent reminder concerning the verse Mark 13:4 –" Tell us, when shall these things be? And what [shall be] the sign when all these things shall be fulfilled?" I am so glad I started to pay attention to words and events that were happening in my life to understand my path. Ask yourself what events have happened in your life for you to put together the puzzles that might be missing on your path to unlocking the virtuous woman within you?

I have to admit I was very sad and depressed when my father passed away. I needed those reinforced words of who I was and what I was being formed into, a diamond. Right there, I declared in my hospital bed that I was going to dedicate my life to my father by believing in myself, discovering my purpose and passion and allowing the diamond in me to emerge. The signs saved my life and were the keys that freed me from my mental imprisonment as it reinforced the diamond within me, but put me on a path to help others understand their diamond, (purpose and passion). After that day in the hospital, I found my foundation to move forth, so when other trails, storms, and earthquakes came down my path, I had the tools. Therefore, when I was raped at 27, in a verbally abusive marriage and had to have an urgent hysterectomy done due to uterus cancer, which I am now 8 years in remission. This was part of my equipping as I continued to develop into the diamond in the rough. These earthquakes in my life developed me and are now the tools that create a connection and help others who might have or are going through similar events in their lives. We must be open to the fact that we are a vessel being used to help others discover their diamond so the virtuous women in them can shine. As 2 Timothy 2:21 teaches, **"If a man therefore purge himself from these, he shall be a vessel unto honors, sanctified, and meet for the master's use, [and] prepared unto every good work."**

SUPPLICATION

Father, I thank you in the name of Jesus for giving me the awareness to understand, at a very early age, spiritual signs and to recognize the signs that you gave me to move forth and understand my purpose and passion. I truly know that the path that you chose for me was not my will but your will to strengthen and assist others in understanding how to hear your voice during my trials and tribulation. As the word states in Romans 8:37, "Nay, in all these things we are more than conquerors through him that loved us."

By living and standing on your word, I believe I am more than a conqueror and I can survive what comes my way to refine and remind me of my purpose in you, Lord. My strength does not come from me but from you. I am here because you have a plan You have declared for me to help others. I come against any evil that the enemy wants to aim my way to hinder and have my purpose stand as a positive influence. I thank you, my faithful Father and love, and adore you. In the name of Jesus, I praise your name and offer this prayer. Amen.

AFFIRMATION

I
believe in my purpose.
I am intelligent.
I am more than enough.
I shall not let negative words define me.
I am more than a Conquers.

I can do all things through Christ Jesus.
I am the head and not the tail.
I shall NOT live in fear from others.
I am special in God's eye.

APPLICATION

Look for Signs Towards Your Purpose

It has been stated, "Living a life of purpose can motivate you to get up in the morning and put your full energy into your day Knowing your purpose in life can help you feel as though your routines and habits are meaningful and important to yourself and those around you. You can live a life of purpose by following your passions and by setting goals. You may also find purpose in life by giving back to others and by living a more balanced life, where you appreciate what you have and savor every moment of your day" Carmela Resuma.

Write an "I'm will Not Ignore the Signs Going Towards My Purpose in Life" Proclamation. In this statement, you want to identify what makes you passionate that is moving in your life in a positive manner and would you think the Lord might say to you. In addition, list the purpose (scriptures) according to God.

"I Will Not Ignore the Signs Towards my Purpose in Life" Proclamation:

I will work toward understanding the signs I receive and pray against (Challenge or Opposition)

_____

To Overcome my challenges, I will (solution),

_____

Overcoming Scripture: Write scriptures from the word of God that you can have as a reminder when trusting the signs you receive from seeking your purpose and passion.

_____

Find a person that can be an accountability partner for you to work on increasing your awareness and faith going towards your passion.

_____
_____

ABOUT THE AUTHOR

Professional Keynote Speaker/Author/Co-Founder Diamond Empowerment - Women of Connection Network

Barbara empowers women to overcome their challenges and helps them shine. Growing up in an interracial family in Chicagoland during the tumultuous 1970s imbued her with a bright inner light. This light has fueled her desire to help others. She believes people are people and that colors are there to remind us we all have filters to work through to appreciate the person underneath.

Knowing work and education were keys to success, she began working in insurance at age fifteen. Upon graduating high school, she obtained associates degrees in accounting and computerized business management, business management, and health administrative management. This landed her a job with AON Risk Services Insurance Brokerage in their insurance department.

Wanting to become a better senior manager at AON, she found her true calling by joining a Toastmasters Club. Embracing the Toastmaster's vision of improving communication and leadership skills, she worked her way up to becoming a program quality director, providing educational opportunities for over 5500 Toastmaster's members. The great part is that Barbara is just getting started. At the beginning of 2019, she started the Diamond Empowerment – Women of Connection Network. Barbara's motto: "You have a DIAMOND in you." Let it shine because everyone has something special within them the Diamond Factor equals your Purpose, Passion and Drive as your foundation to encourage a person to move forward despite the trials and challenges in your life.

CONTACT INFORMATION

Email Address: showyourdiamond@gmail.com

Website: www.BarabaraBeckley.com

SOCIAL MEDIA

Facebook Page: DiamondFactorBB group

DESTINED -TO BRING GOD GLORY
Gwen Bennett

Jesus answered, "Everyone who drink this water will be thirsty again, but whoever drinks the water that I give them will never thirst. Indeed, the water I give them will become in them a spring of water welling up in to eternal life."
John 4:7-10

There was a lady in scripture, who had no name, but was simply called the Samaritan woman or some even call her the Woman at the well. This woman had come to the well to draw water from Jacob's well. She was probably going about her business doing what she'd probably done hundreds of time before. Little did she know, a divine encounter was going to take place on this day, and her life would forever be changed. The aching, the longing, and the emptiness she felt and had tried to fill with men would be filled by the man and his name was JESUS.

Somewhat like this woman I was empty, only a shadow of who I really was. There was an emptiness inside, and even though I had grew up in the church and asked Christ to come into my life, I was still empty because I never really allowed him to become my Lord. I went through the motions for years. As a young girl I had dreams of going away to attend college. I wanted to be the first of my siblings to become a college graduate. I wanted to work in a Fortune 500 Company, get married, and start a family. However all of my dreams came to an end when I became pregnant while in high school.

As a teenager, I dated the same person on and off during my high school years. The relationship was toxic, but I listened to the devils lies that no one else would ever want me because I was a teenage mom. I bought into that lie and believed it for years, eventually marrying the same person because, in my mind, no one else could ever love or want me.

A short time later, I had two children and a rocky marriage. I tried to be a good wife and mother, but it seemed nothing I did was good enough. I am not saying I was perfect, but I was trying. I was attending church, had rededicated my life to Christ and was really trying to serve him to the best of my ability, praying that he would save my husband and restore my marriage. However, the more I prayed the more abusive the relationship became. In the midst of it all, I was on my way to work one morning, and I heard God say you are going to be a pastor. I laughed. I thought, *No one like me can ever be used to bring God glory or God will never want to use anyone like me.* I never carried many outward bruises, but inside I was a complete mess. I had to get out, if I didn't, someone would be seriously hurt, and it was not only hurting and destroying us but our children. So, then came the D word....DIVORCE. I married to be married forever, so I thought I was a failure. I blamed GOD. I walked away from all I knew (the church). I wanted absolutely nothing to do with God or the church because He let me down.

I tried going to the club, only to get sick as soon as I walked in a sat down at the bar. I would go to parties, only to end up back at home on the sofa crying myself to sleep. I eventually got into another relationship, and it was all going good, so I thought. We were buying a house together and playing a role that God intended for marriage only. I felt like I was in a great relationship because it was totally different from the last, but one day, I ended up at the well, and he reminded me that He chose me I didn't choose Him.

God will put you in a position that will baffle the minds of others. Don't be dismayed, and don't back away. You are destined for greatness.

I soon realized that there was no reason for me to continue fighting this fight, a fight I knew I could never win. There was a conflict between my flesh and my spirit man. It was apparent I had to make a choice. I could continue being frustrated, torn, and empty. I needed help and I needed it fast. I remember writing a prayer request on paper, burning it and burying it. Needless to say, God didn't answer it the way I expected. When he met me at the point of my need like that woman at the well, he asked me some questions, and I had to make some crucial decisions, decisions that would cost me everything: my home, my relationship, and my finances. But I had to trust God. I simply walked away. I didn't know how I was going to make it, but that wasn't my problem, it was Gods now. It wasn't easy, but with God's help, I made it. He helped me to realize he had always been there.

I heard a song on the radio one morning by Martha Munizzi that said, "I just want YOU." When I heard it, I felt like she had peeked into my soul and sang all of the words I wanted to say. Those were the words I was feeling but just couldn't seem to articulate them. I started going back to church. At first, I would ease in and sit in the very back and leave as soon as it was over. But one Sunday, it didn't matter how far back I sat. The Holy Spirit found me, and it was like a dam burst, the flood gates opened, and I felt a breaking, a healing and deliverance from the depth of my soul.

I decided Satan couldn't have me. He couldn't have my kids. Even though my mind was made up, and I had rededicated my life to Christ, that didn't stop Satan from his attacks. He brought attacks against my children, my finances, and my family, but I was in it to win it. I was determined that God was going to be gloried even in the midst of the assaults. I prayed more fervently. My prayers went from begging Him to thanking Him. I learned how to praise in the midst of the pain. In the midst of losing, I was still winning. Did I always feel like praying? Did I always feel like praising? Did I always feel like going on? Certainly not, but I knew I had to. I knew this thing I was feeling inside was far greater than what I was experiencing at the present moment. When I needed strength, I drew from the well.

Days, months and years went by from the time I heard God speak to me and nothing happened. It seemed like everyone around me was getting blessed, or someone was being prophesied to about something concerning their lives and what God was going to do through them. I would see this and wonder, *why don't God ever have a word for me?* I wondered if what I heard was true or if it was just me. I knew I didn't tell myself that because that was nothing I ever wanted to do. I am a very shy person, and I don't like speaking in front of people so to tell myself I was going to pastor, I knew that wasn't a thought from me. Therefore, I just held on to what I knew was God. But it didn't happen overnight. If it had, I would have messed some people up because my lifestyle and character was not intact and certainly not God like. But God kept pruning, and crushing, and when I thought I was ready, I would get smashed again. I would be crushed again, put in the furnace of affliction. It felt as though I was isolated from others. And I had those WHY GOD WHY? days. Why are you allowing me to hurt? Why are you allowing me to experience all of this loneliness. Why do I feel abandoned? You told me at the well that this water would be springing up inside of me. Is there not joy, peace, happiness, comfort in this water? I know I have everlasting life, but what about my life now? Can't I experience some of that abundant life you say I can have? Satan then started telling me lies that I would never be that, and no one wanted to hear me. He would whisper, "You've never been to college, or seminary. you are not qualified." The list goes on and on. He knew where my insecurities were and tried to capitalize on those areas as well. But God!!!

The pastor started preaching a sermon series titled "Kingdom Journey to Purpose," and boy did it open up my eyes as to who I was in God and how God has chosen me. It began to show me how my experience over time had shaped me in some way or another. So one day, I sat down and asked God to show me why I felt a certain way about myself, and when did all of the insecurities start. I sat there that Saturday until God took me back to when it all started. He then reminded me, "I never told you that. You've allowed Satan to rent and occupy space in your mind all these years but today I've come to make you free."

What if the thing that produces your pain is the thing God uses to release His power?

From that sermon series, I begin to realize and see who I was. I came to understand I was destined to bring God glory. Out of all the hurt, the feelings of abandonment, the loneliness, the rejections, and the insecurity, I began believing that I had to go through it to get me here. Here, I did not expect to meet a man who would change my life forever. Here is the place where no one else would see me for who I really am. Here is where they only saw the surface. Here is where I put on my mask, pretending to be happy, to have it all together. But it was here where the mask came off, and the real me was revealed. I was a daughter of the Most High God. Chosen by Him to be a voice for Him to let others know that He makes all things new; he's a restorer and when others devalue you and toss you away, He's a SALVAGING GOD. He finds treasure in what others discard as trash or invaluable. **It is what it is, but with God it's not what it seems. Where you see failure God sees a new future. Where you see rejection God sees refinement.**

I want to encourage you today to know that it does not matter what you may be facing, God is for you. If God has ever spoken a word to you concerning anything, whether it's a business opportunity, your healing, your finances, a call to ministry, marriage, or given birth, hold on to that word. No you might not have it all together, and no you might not be the likely candidate. Your life might be "jacked up" or raggedy right now, but when you least expect it, HE's going to show up. He will begin to show you the real you, not to condemn you, but to bring about Holy conviction that will allow you to become vulnerable, and you will open up in areas you've been keeping closely guarded. I am a pretty secret person; I hate going to the doctor. Well, I don't mind going, but I hate having to get undressed for the examination. One time I was hurting so bad I didn't care about exposing myself. All I know is I wanted the pain to stop. And that's how it's going to be when you have the encounter with him at the WELL. You are just going to want the pain to stop and the emptiness to go away. So open up, let HIM minister to you so that the living water can begin to fill you, and to heal and restore you, so you can know without a shadow of a doubt that you are **DESTINED TO BRING GOD GLORY.**

ALL THE FORCES OF DARKNESS CANNOT STOP WHAT GOD HAS ORDAINED. ISAIAH 14: 27.

SUPPLICATION:

DEAR LORD,

I'm here with all of my issues and my wavering belief in you and your word. But today I ask that you would give me the faith to take you at your word. That I will begin to trust you even when I can't trace you. From today forward, all the emptiness and longing I have, I will fill then with your word. I am tired of trying to do it in my own strength. I want to overcome and walk in my preordained destiny. I believe it, and I receive it! In the matchless name of Jesus Christ.....Amen.

AFFIRMATION

I trust in the Lord in my tribulation for it brings perseverance and proven character.

I trust in the Lord for His yoke is easy and His burden is light, He gives me rest.

I trust in the Lord for He is faithful and keeps His covenant.

I put my trust in the Lord for He is my refuge, I rest in His shadow, for He is my strength and shield.

I trust in the Lord at all times, for He is my Hope. He has great plans for my future, I am called according to His purpose, and He works all things together for my good.

APPLICATION

TRUST: PROVERBS 3:5

To trust in God is to believe that He loves you and that He's got everything in control. He wants to help you. Trust when you can't see or understand what's going on.

I WILL TRUST PROCLAMATION:

❖ I will trust God when:

_____
_____
_____
_____
_____
_____
_____
_____
_____
_____
_____
_____
_____

❖ I have a problem trusting God with: (Be Honest)

_____
_____
_____
_____
_____
_____
_____
_____
_____
_____
_____
_____
_____
_____

Victory Scripture: And we know that all things work together for good to them that love God, to them who are the called according to his purpose. Rom 8:28.

ABOUT THE AUTHOR

On February 8, 2013, Gwen Bennett's world drastically changed after losing a pastor, a mentor and life-long friend. Due to the recent unfortunate, untimely passing of the senior pastor of Faith Free Full Gospel Church, Bennett is now the new senior pastor of Faith Free. "I didn't expect for it to happen like this," Bennett stresses in response to her propel into pastorship. However, because of the mentor-mentee relationship between Bennett and Stamper, she feels that he prepared her well to become a pastor because he gave her the ins and outs, do's and don'ts and taught her proper pastor etiquette.

Gwen Bennett is a native of Buford, GA, a city in which she describes as "modern-country," where she currently serves as a community leader. Gwen has two children, Antwane Bennett, and Kristen (Brandon)King; four grandchildren: Ja'Maya, Jayla, Amir and Braedon. She has been employed with State Farm Insurance for 20 years.

Bennett has been a licensed minister since 2004 and was ordained in 2006 as an Elder and in 2013 as Sr. Pastor. She would dream about ministering but literally heard God say, "You will become the pastor" as she drove to work early one morning. She laughed at the notion. Pastor Gwen knew it was God because she is shy, an introvert, who has always felt more comfortable singing in front of people as opposed to standing up and speaking to them. Bennett believes that some of the common stereotypes about pastors is that they are all perfect, they know everything and they are all about the money. Her stance on these misconceptions is "I don't know everything and I'm not perfect."

When Pastor Bennett is not working, serving her church through Sunday morning services, teaching Bible study or participating in Friday night prayer, she enjoys reading books from many different authors. She especially enjoys spending time and playing with her four grandchildren.

CONTACT INFORMATION

Email Address: gbsacred07@icloud.com

SOCIAL MEDIA

Facebook Page: Pastor Gwen Bennett

HOW TO FORGIVE WHEN HURT BY GOD'S ANOINTED?

Jacqueline Goodwin

"She openeth her mouth with wisdom; and in her tongue is the law of kindness." **Proverbs 31:26:**

Wisdom is needed when dealing with hurt. According to Proverbs 18:22, "Whoso findeth a wife findeth a good thing and obtaineth favor of the Lord." As ordained by God, the man must find the wife before marriage is to take place. As men and women of God seek to get married, they go through the process of dating. During this process of dating, God's anointed may fail to uphold a promise. He may deceive you with lies and manipulation. He may disclose a secret you shared in confidence or even turn his back on you. He may lead you astray from God and the purpose God has called you to do. To sum this up, God's anointed may cause a deep betrayal that will paralyze you from moving forward in your destiny. Relationships consist of having sunshine and rain; however, when God's anointed is involved in a relationship, particularly with another one of God's chosen vessels, the relationship carries a different kind of weight. When leaders are dating and things go wrong within the relationship, we cannot become vicious and seek to destroy God's anointed. Therefore, the question arises, "How do I forgive when hurt by God's anointed?"

First, let's take a look at the word "betrayal." Betrayal is not a problem if you are betrayed by your enemy. It is painful when it is done by a love one. The problem arises when the relationship does not work, and the wounded individual does not know how to heal. Who can the individual talk to that will not change how other's view God's anointed? Therefore, one must be careful when seeking counsel in such a delicate matter. It is important and wise to seek God first so He may guide you to godly counsel. Betrayal is painful within normal relationships without either party being in a leadership role. However, when both parties are in leadership roles it opens a wound that is unbearably deep. Nevertheless, when you are dealing with God's anointed, it should not be taken lightly.

The two main elements in relationships are emotional attachment and respect. So, when we are wounded by God's anointed, we sometimes react through retaliation and attacking. For example, when your dog, who loves you, is hit by a car would attack you because he is in pain. He retaliates because he does not see beyond his pain. When we have been wounded by God's anointed, we cannot see beyond our pain. We place such high standards on God's elect that when he makes a mistake our flesh naturally wants to destroy him. However, that is not how we as Proverbs women of God should resolve the issue.

As one of God's anointed, I struggled with forgiving another one of God's elect because of betrayal. I thought there was a difference between God's anointed and the men of the world. God does expect there to be a difference according to Romans 12:2: "And be not conformed to this world: but be ye transformed by the renewing of your mind, that ye may prove what is that good, and acceptable, and perfect, will of God." We as women of God sometimes get into relationships prematurely which causes pain. Instead, we should wait on the man who God has to ordain for us. The purpose of God's anointed being equally yoked is to operate ministries as God had established the foundation of marriage in love and unity. Even though I have this revelation, I must still deal with the pain that now resides inside of me.

I remember many days crying before God asking how I will move forward and get beyond my pain. God began to reveal several steps for me to take. The first step I had to take was to acknowledge to myself that I was hurt. Secondly, I had to acknowledge to God's anointed that he hurt me. That was easier said than done. To be honest, I simply did not want to see the individual again. My solution was out of sight and out of mind, but it was not the right solution because according to Mark 11:25, "And when ye stand praying, forgive if ye have ought against any that your Father also which is in heaven may forgive you your trespasses."

Instead of keeping my pain bottled up on the inside, I had to release it and so should you. Release your pain appropriately and respectably. David confronted Saul as to why he wanted to kill him and like David, we should confront God's anointed with love and inform him of the pain that has been caused. Always pray and fast to allow God to show you when and how to confront His elect because we do not want to be led by our emotions, but by the spirit of God according to Romans 8:5: "For they that are after the flesh do mind the things of the flesh, but they that are after the Spirit mind the things of the Spirit." God may lead you to contact the individual by letter or a phone call, but if you are in your flesh, you will miss God's guidance and instructions. It is often Satan's attempts to use our pain that has been caused by God's anointed to destroy him, but that is not God. God has given us a commandment in how to approach God's anointed. According to 1 John 4:21, "And this commandment have we from him, that he would loveth God love his brother also." God is love and as women of God, we must govern ourselves with that same love toward His elect.

Even after acknowledging my pain to myself and God's anointed, I had to consistently pray for God to heal my brokenness. The pastor I was dating chose to be involved with other women while we were seeing each other, so this was a very painful experience for me because I developed trust issues as well as insecurities. I sought God daily to put the correct words in my mouth even when I spoke about his anointed vessel because the pain was fresh, and it hurt me to the core. I never imagined a man of God wounding me in that capacity because I was used to the men of the world cheating, lying, and manipulating. Even though you and I may have been hurt by God's anointed, it is the glory of being God's chosen vessel not to be like all the other women who seek revenge to destroy him, but react as God would expect His Proverbs 31 Woman to respond with wisdom, kindness, and compassion. I encourage you, when you are attempted to react out of your pain, to look to the hills from which comes your help, and trust God enough not to take hostile actions against the man of God, even when you have the opportunity. Apostle Paul tells us in 1 Thessalonians 5:11: "Wherefore comfort yourselves together, and edify one another, even as also ye do." In other words, we should encourage God's anointed despite the pain he caused us once we have gone through the process of forgiving and releasing him. Never tear him down but build him up, that through this pain that both of you can grow and use it to minister to others. I am finding the purpose in my pain, and I pray as you continue to read my chapter that you will discover the purpose in your hurt by God's anointed.

The second step God revealed to me was "Do not Put Your Hand or Mouth Against His Anointed." He took me to 1 Samuel 24:10, "Behold, this day thine eyes have seen how that the Lord had delivered thee today in mine hand in the cave: and some bade me kill thee: but mine eye spared thee; and I said, I will not put forth mine hand against my lord; for he is the Lord's anointed."

David experienced the betrayal of God's anointed, King Saul. Saul became fill with jealousy until the point of wanting to kill David, yet David would not touch God's anointed with hands nor his mouth. What a powerful tool for us Proverbs Women to apply in our situation. Yes, even in the midst of betrayal, rejection, manipulation, and lies, we must have the spirit of David and not take matters into our own hand. David respected the God-given office of Saul despite the man Saul became. It takes God living inside and abiding within us to look beyond the pain caused by His anointed vessel and respect his God-given office. Would we dare to say that David forgave Saul for trying on many occasions to kill him? Yes, David forgives Saul.

As I shared that I was betrayed by one of God's anointed, but like David, I had to respect his God-given office. I looked beyond my pain to see the call on his life. Yes, it was painful for me to focus on ministry, but it is not impossible. Betrayal is as deadly as poison if not handled and confronted appropriately. Betrayal can destroy the ministry that God has placed in you if you do not allow God to heal you. As I reflect upon my experience of being hurt by God's anointed, I am reminded of how I wanted to stop attending church. The pain seemed unbearable for me to focus and operate effectively in my God-given office as a prophetess. I asked myself how God's anointed can hurt another one of God's chosen vessels. With tears pouring down my face, I sought God diligently, asking how the place could where I am to be healed and restored hurt me. I asked God, "Is this how the ministry operates?" I began to take the pain that God's anointed caused me and project it on to churches, which was not right. It is very easy for the enemy to come in during our time of pain and cause us to misplace our pain. It was not the church who hurt me, but one person. So, I had to place my hurt in the right place for God to begin healing me. God took me to Psalm 34:18, "The Lord is nigh unto them that are of a broken heart; and saveth such as be of a contrite spirit." God was with me even through this painful experience. It was God who was going to heal my broken heart, and He is going to do the same for you. As I sought God more, I realized that in spite of the pain His anointed caused me I still had to forgive and love him. God began to show me that though Saul betrayed David, he refused to stretch forth his hand against Saul when he had opportunities to do so. However, David allowed Saul to live. I realized I had several opportunities to retaliate and spiritually kill God's anointed's character, but all I could hear was 1 Samuel 24:10. Though my flesh wanted God's anointed to feel the pain I was going through, I knew causing him the pain was not the answer.

I learned through my betrayal that only God can truly bring forth deliverance from pain that is caused by His anointed vessel. He will in due time confront him and deal with him accordingly. You can never accomplish or gain anything by tearing down or destroying God's anointed. The power of death and life is in our tongue. David never spoke death upon Saul, and we should never speak death over God's anointed. As you start to speak life upon God's anointed you will begin to feel a sense of freedom from the pain he caused you. The more I prayed for the pastor I felt a burden being lifted off my shoulder. God would have me pray for him daily speaking life over him, praying for his healing, and declaring a blessing upon his life. This was not an easy task for me, but I did it persistently. God revealed to me, "Pain is necessary and without it, healing does not exist!" These tools led me to fast and pray which I will discuss in another chapter.

SUPPLICATION

Heavenly Father, today I come to you to stop and allow you to come in to heal my broken heart. I no longer want to mask nor sweep my pain under the rug and bury it. I come asking you to heal my broken heart by going into the areas I have allowed darkness to reside. You are the true vine that holds my healing, and as I am one of the branches, your healing shall flow to me as I stay connected to you removing the blindness from my eyes that I may see the truth. Lord, my heart, mind, and soul have been wounded and damaged. I need you to come in and perfect them by removing the layers of bitterness, hate, unforgiveness, and resentment by creating in me a clean heart. I seal this prayer with the blood of Jesus and in His name! Amen!

AFFIRMATION

Recite these affirmations daily!

I will be kind, and compassionate to God's anointed, forgiving him, just as Christ, God forgave me! Ephesians 4:32

I will forgive God's anointed so that I will be forgiven. Luke 6:37

I will clothe myself with compassion, kindness, humility, gentleness, and patience. Bear with God's anointed and forgive whatever grievances I have against him. Colossians 3:12-13.

I will not seek revenge or bear a grudge against God's anointed but love him as myself. Leviticus 19:18.

I will not let any unwholesome talk come out of my mouth, but only what helps build God's anointed to his needs, that it may benefit those who listen. Ephesians 4:29.

APPLICATION

1.   Name the person who wounded you. Here is where you say their name out loud, so it becomes real to you.

2. Identify the way you are acknowledging your hurt: Healthy or Unhealthy.

3. Here are the healthy ways to acknowledge your hurt: look beneath the surface, be painfully honest, and unmask your hurt.

4. Looking beneath the surface, you need to ask yourself what issues am I facing today because of being hurt by God's anointed? (shame, insecurities, low self-esteem, suicidal thoughts, anger, etc).

5. Being painfully honest, identify the act that God's anointed has done to wound you (cheating, lying, manipulating, etc.).

ABOUT THE AUTHOR

Jacqueline Goodwin is an ordained pastor and prophetess whose ministry focus is deliverance and healing. She has a passion and heart for the youth, which has led her to various positions within the ministry and career field. Since 2002 Goodwin has served as Youth Director, a mentor, and Sunday School teacher within her local church. A former paralegal, educator, and substance abuse counselor who used her gift of empowerment to transform lives within her career field. She has earned a Master of Arts in Practical Theology from Regent University, Master of Counseling from Webster University, Columbia SC, a Master of Pastoral Counseling from Liberty University, Lynchburg VA, an Associate Degree of Paralegal graduating "Magna Cum Laude" from South University and a Bachelor of Arts in English from Francis Marion University, Florence SC.

She currently resides in South Carolina with her son, two daughters and granddaughter. Her hobbies include running, walking, meditating, and writing, counseling youth and working in the community.

CONTACT INFORMATION

Email Address: Jacquelinegoodwin0507@gmail.com

Website: www.healinginthevesselministries.com

SOCIAL MEDIA

Twitter: @Jacquel58497682

Facebook Page: @lenisegoodwin

Instagram: @lenisegoodwin

GUARD YOUR HOUSEHOLD

Derashay Zorn

---

*She watches over the ways of her household, And
does not eat the bread of idleness.*

Proverbs 31:27

The watchmen set guard high up in the watchtower observing everything in sight. From the north, south, east, and west, their eyes go to and fro catching everything within one's peripheral view. Leaving nothing unnoticed or unguarded from any potential dangers or threats and attacks from the enemy. Watchmen's understand the importance of their responsibility as individuals, towns, kingdoms, and nations depend on their alertness. An unguarded moment could place everyone within its unwatched territory in immediate danger. Causing those within its borders scrambling for survival. Therefore, they do not leave their post unattended as they anticipate the moment of having to sound the alarm when a potential enemy is spotted afar.

A watchman reminds me of an eagle who can spot their prey from miles away. Just as the eagle can locate their prey from miles away, so does a virtuous woman spot potential threats and danger approaching her territory. She leaves nothing to chance as she is very protective over what God has entrusted to her.

A virtuous woman is known to possess the same skillsets and responsibilities as a watchman. She is very in tuned with everything that is taking place within her household as she governs everything accordingly. She doesn't waste her time with activities that do not lead to the productivity or protection of her family. The virtuous woman doesn't stand guard from a place of insecurity but from a place of responsibility.

In Genesis 21:8-10, we will find Sarah protecting her son Isaac from his older brother Ishmael. One day, Abraham prepared a feast after the weaning of Isaac. During the feast, Sarah noticed Ishmael consistently being very mean unto Isaac. This concerned Sarah as she watched Ishmael act out his anger toward Isaac. She saw the threat that Ishmael posed to her son and she went into action. Sarah spoke to Abraham and requested for Ishmael to be removed from their camp. I'm sure she probably wavered with the impact that this would have on Abraham as well as Ishmael. However, her concern was the long-term impact that it could have on Isaac's life. His life was of greater importance.

A virtuous woman can learn a lot from Sarah in these few verses. Her concern was the welfare of her household and God's promise for it. This should be the concern of every woman, single or married. We cannot allow our desires for the comfort of others to disrupt or pose a threat to our household. This would also mean pursuing our very own desires that pose a threat to what God has entrusted in us. We cannot be so caught up with people, places, or things that it leaves our household open to demonic influencers. We cannot be so caught up in ourselves that the television and the streets are raising our children. Neither can we desire a man so much that it sabotages the future of our children, as they are put in harm's way just so we can gratify the desire of our flesh. Sarah made a bold decision by putting Isaac's wellbeing first. We can also find Pilate's wife interfering with government affairs for the sake of her household.

In the book of Matthew, we find Pilate's wife being a watchman over the affairs of her household and bringing forth the warning necessary to eliminate her family from suffering any consequences of a poor decision. It also indicates that she had some form of relationship with God as she was given insight on the matter at hand. Not only did she have a dream that she understood but it also compelled her to sound the alarm. I'm sure it was not customary for the wives to interfere with the affairs of the government; however, there was something great at stake. At this time, what the government was doing became a part of her business because it was a threat to her household.

> YOUR STATUS IN THE WORLD CANNOT MEAN MORE TO YOU THEN YOUR STATUS WITH GOD. YOU MUST NOT SEEK THE INTEREST OF SELFISH GAIN AND LEAVE YOUR FAMILY VULNERABLE TO DANGER.
>
> -DR. DERASHAY ZORN

"While he was sitting on the judgment seat, his wife sent to him, saying, "Have nothing to do with that just Man, for I have suffered many things today in a dream because of Him." Matthew 27:19

Therefore, she responded by sending word to her husband, the Roman governor of Judea, warning him to have nothing to with the death of Jesus. God spoke to Pilate's wife in her dreams about Jesus in hopes that she could warn and reach her husband before he made a terrible mistake. She gives him this warning because she had a dream about Jesus, and she had suffered much in her dream. She also understood from her dream that Jesus was a just man, and it would be innocent bloodshed if He were executed. Therefore, it would be wised that her husband let Him go so that they would not be affected by his decision.

Her words about Jesus' innocence was known unto him. Pilate declares Jesus was not guilty of what he was being charged, three-times. In spite of what he knew and the warning of his wife, his decision was not weighed on truth, but his political struggle and the people's popular demands. This was very unfortunate for him because he overlooked his wife's warning in the matter.

As a virtuous woman, we must watch over the affairs of our home and be willing to speak up and take a stand against anything that becomes a potential threat. When wrong decisions are about to be made that could be of danger to your household, your voice matters. Pilate's wife's voice wasn't led by her emotions, but it was led by the Spirit of God to protect her home. She was not concerned about the political, prosperity or popularity gain that it would have brought to her household. Her concern was their status with God and not man.

When we become focused on social and economic status, we tend to look the other way and omit justice. We leave our post and put our entire household in danger. This happens when we have not decided to truly serve God. In our decision to serve God, we stand on and up for His word. We don't mind going against what is popular for what is right. Even if this means speaking up to our husbands and standing against their affairs that threaten our household.

In the book of Ezekiel chapter 33, God told Ezekiel, I have called you a watchman, and you shall hear a word from my mouth and warn them for me." Pilate's wife did just that. And we should follow the same order. Ezekiel was told, if he was given a warning by God and failed to provide the warning, the person would die in their iniquity, but their blood would be required at Ezekiel's hand. When watchmen do not sound the alarm, it leaves whatever they are guarding in great danger and ultimately they become responsible for not following through with their responsibility. A virtuous woman understands that if she doesn't sound the alarm when the enemy appears, she puts her household in danger. So, she does not mind being vocal and standing against anything that stands against the word of God.

To be a faithful watchman over her household, the virtuous woman must have an authentic relationship with God. Out of her relationship with God, she governs the affairs of her household. This keeps her from showing partiality, being passive, and operating from her emotions. As she watches over her home and everything, she weighs every matter against the word of God. And she allows His word to be authoritative over all affairs.

As a watchman of her home, she intercedes on behalf of it. She knows how to forward all matters unto God and waits on His response before she reacts. This keeps her emotions in check and keeps her from making decisions she would later regret. Every choice she makes is for the protection and preservation of her family. It saves her family from danger because she is grounded in Christ.

Her relationship with God keeps her knowledgeable of her family affairs. God provides her with wisdom on matters that are taken place in her absence, so she can handle any opposing threat to her household. In a dream, Pilate's wife was informed of the affairs of her husband by God because it posed a threat to her family. And she was able to warn him in spite of him not listening. Also, in 1 Samuel 25, God used Abigail's servant to inform her of how Nabal, her husband, treated David and the threat it brought upon her household.

Her quick response saved her household as she met David and his army before they could make it to her home and kill every male within it. David eluded her intelligent and quick thinking unto the Lord. *"Then David said to Abigail: "Blessed is the LORD God of Israel, who sent you this day to meet me! And blessed is your advice and blessed are you, because you have kept me this day from coming to bloodshed and from avenging myself with my own hand. For indeed, as the LORD God of Israel lives, who has kept me back from hurting you, unless you had hastened and come to meet me, surely by morning light no males would have been left to Nabal!"* 1 Samuel 25:32-34. "

Abigail didn't waste any time with taken care of this matter and that included going to her husband to attempt to convince him so that he could correct it. She knew he was stubborn, would not listen and that the consequences would have failed them by the time he might have wanted to hear her. She was led by God on how to move and when to save her household.

When it comes to the wellbeing of our household, we should not be slothful in our response to deal with a matter. Our response should be of importance because we care about our family's future, and desires for every one of God's word to come to pass. Every day, the virtuous woman stands on post guarding the ways of her household and God's purpose for it.

WHEN WATCHMEN DO NOT SOUND THE ALARM, IT LEAVES WHATEVER THEY ARE GUARDING IN GREAT DANGER AND ULTIMATELY THEY BECOME RESPONSIBLE FOR NOT FOLLOWING THROUGH WITH THEIR RESPONSIBILITY.

-DR. DERASHAY ZORN

SUPPLICATION:

Dear Heavenly Father,

I come before your throne with a heart of thanksgiving and a mouth full of praise. I want to thank you for giving me the responsibility of a watchman. I thank you I am equipped to stand guard and sound the alarm. As a watchman, I ask that you forgive me for every time I have abandon my post and put my household in danger in the name of Jesus. I thank you for being a forgiving and loving God. Now, I ask that you give me greater insight and train me so I can appropriately carry out every duty that is required of me.

In the name of Jesus, I ask for your strength to stay on duty and the wisdom to actively engage in the spiritual forces that stand against my household. Clothe me in your armor that I may withstand the wales of the evil one. Guard my mind that I may not be deceived, and guide my feet that I may walk in the counsel of your ways.

In the name of Jesus, repair every wall that has been broken in my household and left us vulnerable to the attacks of the enemy. I stand this day to take my post and never leave it again. Father, sharpen my eyes and ears that I may hear and see the enemy afar. Give me the faith to sound the alarm and not withhold anything. I rebuke the spirit of intimidation and fear right now in the name of Jesus. God, I thank you for training my hands to battle and providing me with the tools to slay the enemy every time he launches an attack, in the name of Jesus. I thank you for equipping me to be a spiritual snipper and that threats are quickly taken out before they come near the tent of my dwellings in the name of Jesus.

I thank you for the sake of my family I am bold as a lion, gentle as a dove, and wise as a serpent. That nothing will get pass my gates to cause harm to my household. I thank you that my home is fortified in you and that daily you provide the provisions necessary to keep it secure from danger. I thank you for giving me the ear of those within my household that they trust the words from my lips as they come from your heart. I praise your holy name that nothing will supersede the importance of my home. In the majestic name of Jesus, I pray. Amen, Amen, and Amen.

AFFIRMATION

I am a watchman over my household.

I will not be afraid to speak up for what's right.

I will take a stand against anything that threatens my home.

I am responsible and accountable for the affairs of my household.

I will protect my home, children, and family.

I will take a stand for righteousness.

I will intercede on behalf of my household.

I will only make godly decisions.

Out of my mouth shall flow the wisdom of God.

I shall sound the alarm when God speaks.

My family will not be a victim of my emotions.

I shall be actively engaged in every area of my family's affairs.

I shall not be idle.

APPLICATION

FAMILY VISION BOARD

1. Do a family vision board.

2. Develop a SWOT analysis for your household.

3. What are your areas strength, weaknesses, growth and family threats?

4. Develop a plan of action to optimize your strengths in targeting your other areas of development that strengthen your areas of weakness, mature in your areas of growth opportunities, and eliminate all threats.

5. Pray over the affairs of your household daily.

6. Keep a pray journal concerning your home and family vision.

7. Know the vision for your family and its course before you.

8. Keep your heart and ears open to what God is speaking concerning your household.

9. Talk with those within your home about their portion in the family vision to keep the vision before them and help them stay on task. If any concerns arise, let then know and give advice as needed so they can stay focused toward their part in the family over the vision. When making a decision, measure it up against the word of God. And let the word of God be the determining factor.

10. Plan family meetings with intentional conversations about your family's future. Talk to them on the family progress, celebrate, correct, and help one another in assignment.

ABOUT THE AUTHOR

Kingdom Strategist, Blueprint Builder, and Spiritual Midwife, **Dr. Derashay Zorn** is an international business coach and expert in the art of **unleashing purpose, developing dreams, and expanding untapped potentials within individuals, corporations, and ministries.** Her passion for information technology has led her to obtain a Master of Science in Information System Management which equipped her to **specialize in analyzing, developing and managing systems to birth or expand individuals and entities into the next dimension of kingdom implementation.**

Derashay equips mankind globally as the Founder of the **Kingdom Influencers Network, In The Church™ TV & Radio Broadcast, Divine Order Restoration Ministries (D.O.R.M) International, Kingdom Strategist Firm, Women of Influence Magazine, (D.O.R.M) Publishing** and many other entrepreneurship endeavors that equip mankind globally. Through, her global brands **Kingdom Strategies University® & School of Authorpreneur®**, .she teaches others **how to maximize their potential and monetize their gifts and talents** as a critical vehicle for fulfilling their purpose, making a significant impact and branding influence that can instantly and beautifully change the world. Her books and workbook titled **"Abortions In the Church: Divine Strategies to Spiritual Deliverance" & Meant for My Good: Being Developed In The Midst of the Disaster** is helping others overcome and give birth to their purpose, visions, and dreams. She is a wife, mother, pastor, entrepreneur; consultant, empowerment speaker, mentor, and friend.

Her philosophy is **"A critical tool for self-development is learning how to cultivate, build and release others into their destinies."**

CONTACT INFORMATION

Email Address: info@derashayzorn.com

Website: www.derashayzorn.com

SOCIAL MEDIA

Twitter: @kbstrategist

Facebook Page: @kingdombusinessstrategist

Instagram: @kingdomstrategist

SAY NOT I AM A CHILD

Temecka Smith

Then the word of the Lord came unto me, saying,
Before I formed thee; and before thou camest forth
out of the womb I sanctified thee, and I ordained
thee a prophet unto the nations. Then said I, Ah,
Lord God! Behold, I cannot speak: For I am a child.
But the Lord said unto me, Say not, I am a child: For
thou shalt go to all that I shall send thee, and
whatsoever I command thee thou shalt speak.
Jeremiah 1:4-7

This year I will be walking into the forty fifth chapter in the book of my life, and from the very first chapter until now I have made it through events and circumstances that stand as a daily reminder to me of God's enduring love. Many times, when you have a purpose set on your life by God, the enemy attempts to take you out as early as possible, and my life is living proof that this is true. The enemy didn't waste any time in making an effort to stop God's plans for my life. In my mother's womb my life became threatened by a rare bacteria that got in my blood. I was miraculously healed because of her relentless prayers. I often say, "Weapons formed against your life at a young age is evidence of a person who God wants to use for His glory."

While growing up, my innocence was violated, which started to shape and morph the way I saw myself and viewed life. These events left me broken, and just as so many women do I began to search out my identity in relationships. Being beautiful in a man's eyes became my definition of worth. I started chasing the love the world could give me in hopes of filling the void of wanting to be a daddy's little girl. Most of the world is on a search for wholeness that only the Father in heaven can give.

During that season of my life, I appeared to have it all together, and in the world's eyes I was prospering. But, I didn't realize the more I started to gain the world, the more I was losing who God called me to be. I would hear

93

Him calling me, but I would drown Him out with the life I was creating. We so often ignore the knocks from God on our hearts. So many times God is calling us to surrender the easy way, but we choose the harder way. Becoming pregnant at seventeen was my biggest blessing and honestly saved my life. Having my baby girl shifted my focus off of myself and on to the fact that her life was in my hands. God used motherhood to rescue me from myself. Motherhood started the shift in my life, but it still wasn't when I fully surrendered.

As I stated earlier, I knew clearly I had a call on my life, but my plans were still drowning out His. I have to point out that I have grown up in church my whole life, and I am so thankful for that because even in the messiness of it all I still had a foundation to come back to. Soon I would find out how critical that foundation would be. I found myself surrounded by bullets flying as I ran, and not one touched me. I want to show you that God wants us to surrender willfully, but He knows what it will take for us to fall on our knees. I know, with all my heart, if I would have obeyed the many times He had called me before, I would have never had to have that experience. But God knows what it will take. The fire of the process is what it takes to become all that God has called you to be. If there was ever a man who made nations tremble with his words and allowed God to use him to shake kingdoms, his name was Jerimiah. One of the major prophets, better known as the weeping prophet, who unequivocally walked in the authority that he had been given somehow still managed to have hesitation in his capabilities. This great man clearly had his share of insecurities and was well acquainted with the feeling of inadequacy. When one reads about his strengths and the capacity of how he was used by God, it certainly makes grasping that Jeremiah would ever doubt his ability to walk out what God had called him to do difficult and hard to believe.

Studying one of the greatest prophets reveals the underlying whisper of the character of God, and you begin to uncover the comforting truth that He doesn't need a perfect person, only a willing vessel with an obedient heart. How many times have you heard the prompting of the Holy Spirit but quickly drowned out His voice with your own resounding list of your limitations? When we are being called to do something that surpasses our level of confidence, we are very swift in giving God another solution. We often refer to our contact list secretly tucked in our mind of people who we consider superior in spiritual stature. I guarantee you the name of that person on your more dignified list just came to the forefront of your mind.

What if I told you that God does not want your vote for the most likely to succeed? Please take no offense, but if God would brush off Jeremiah's worried hearts cry, He isn't paying yours much attention either. Everyone wants to identify with the powerfully anointed words of Jeremiah. You know the ones about having plans to prosper and not plans to harm you, but have you ever found yourself more acquainted with His plea to God that he was only a child? We are powerful women of God; however, if we are honest, sometimes we can't get beyond the messy places in our lives and we, more often than we would like to admit, find ourselves rejecting what our father sees in us. My friend, you are not alone in those vulnerable moments of insecurity. I have been there and Jeremiah was there too during those moments when God was calling you to walk through doors that your weaknesses say you will never enter.

Our stories may differ in names, places, and events but if you listen our journeys will sound familiar. First, let me say, when you are called by God, the foremost goal of the enemy is to break you down so that you never find your identity in Christ. Often times, He will start as early as your childhood to cause confusion in whom you have been called to be. That's where he started in my life. He stole my innocence at an early age and used other doors that led to brokenness. From trauma to teen pregnancy and everything in between these events began to shape the way I viewed myself and they clouded the lenses I saw life through. I began to question my worth and value. Instead of allowing God's words to define me, The voice of man became the loudest voice that I could hear. The attention of man gave me value and the seed from the enemy in my mind was planted. But God is so rich in mercy that He will use what the enemy meant for bad and turn it around for our good.

As I walked with this belief for many seasons, the voice of God was becoming more and more distant. Who was I? The more I placed man's labels on me the further I was walking away from my true identity. In that season, you could not have told me I did not know who I was. To the world's standards, I had it all together, and I had reached the peak of living my best life. However, I found something out quickly. When you have a call on your life and a praying mother, God will only allow you to drown Him out so much until He makes it very clear that you are His.

This was the beginning of my turning point. Even though, I seemed unbreakable from the outside; on the inside, I was shattering. That's what we often do when we have been through hardships in life. We create a hard shell to mask what is really going on inside. I appeared to be very secure

HE STOLE MY INNOCENCE

in myself, but truthfully I had layers of insecurities. I came to a place where I was tired of being a puppet for others. I decided to go back to the foundation of who I was. I grew up in church, and I knew enough about God to know that He had something more for me. I had it all worked out that I would live in the fullness of who God called me to be, and I would leave my past behind. This was a cute thought until God started calling me into ministry. I wasn't seeking a title I just wanted God. But like many of you, I found out that God's plans sometimes are bigger than ours. How or why would God ask someone with my past and my pain to wear such big shoes. I didn't fit the cookie cutter ministry shoes. Again, God doesn't want what the world accepts, He wants the rejected and left behind. Daughter, it does not matter if you meet the qualifications or not. God qualified you from your mother's womb. In the natural, I have been in rooms where I know I did not belong.

Let my story encourage you that God is not looking for the greatest. He is seeking out the least of thee. Credentials do not impress Him. if you have been feeling inadequate, please be encouraged that He needs you. When the world counts you out, get excited because He is setting you up for greatness. I tell everyone I am Jesus's little girl and I mean that with all my heart. Jesus gives favor to his daughters. Because He is the best father a girl could ask for, He never breaks a promise. Whatever God is calling you to do right now, breathe and be comforted in knowing he is not measuring you by your ability. When you hear His voice, say not you are just a child but take His hand and know that He is with you.

SUPPLICATION

Father, I repent for all the times that I allowed the whispers of insecurity to stop me from saying yes. I thank you for choosing me and for holding my hand through the difficult seasons of my life. Thank you for your goodness and for your mercy. As I walk into the great plans that you have for me, help me to walk boldly and know that you are in control. Father, when I find myself discouraged, remind me that I am more than the words that people have used to define me. I know that I can do absolutely nothing apart from you, but with you, I can do all things in your name. Heal me from every wound and hidden trauma that made its way into my life. I want to be made whole. Give me the strength to be transparent about what I have been through in order to help others. I realize that everything that I have been through can help lead one of your lost children back to you. My purpose must come forth in the name of Jesus, and I thank you for not allowing me to stay stuck in what is familiar and comfortable. Continue to draw me closer to you, and teach me to abide in your presence. You are my first love, and I completely surrender my mind, will , and emotions to you. I will serve you faithfully all the days of my life. In the name of Jesus, Amen.

AFFIRMATION

I am no longer a victim but always an overcomer.

I clothed in the armor of God daily.

I die to my flesh daily and am lead by your spirit.

No weapon formed against me shall ever prosper.

I am strong in the Lord.

The wisdom of the Lord guides my life.

The peace of God is always upon me, and I am not easily moved.

I am the apple of the Lords eyes.

I am the head and never the tail.

I am faithful over the things that God trusts me with.

When my heart is overwhelmed, He always leads me to a rock.

APPLICATION

Say not I am a child

When we do not know who we are, we allow the enemy and other people to determine who we are and who we can be. We have to actively, every day, remind ourselves of who God has called us to be in order for us to walk out boldly the plans that He has for us. I know how hard it can be to drown out all the other voices. But woman of God, you must be intentional on this walk. Think of every lie the enemy has told you about who you are, and replace it with a truth from God's word about you. In this statement, don't focus on who you are not, but write a declaration of who you are. Be a bold woman of God and prophesy over yourself of who you are and who you are becoming.

God says, I am declaration

I am God's chosen instrument, and I am _____

_____

_____

_____

_____

When I find myself feeling inadequate, instead of giving into that mindset, I choose to do this instead? I

_____

_____

_____

Victory Scripture: Write scriptures from the word of God that you can stand on.

_____

_____

Who can you use as a resource to hold you accountable and hold you up?

_____

ABOUT THE AUTHOR

Temecka Smith is a trailblazer with one goal in mind, to be the hands and feet of Jesus. The hats that she wears are many in number, but preaching the unadulterated truth is in her eyes, the most important. She serves as the associate pastor of **Good Samaritan Center of Hope** planted in Knoxville, Tennessee where she has labored for nine years. She has a passion for seeing lives changed which is made evident as she is the founder of her international ministry **Real Life-Real Issues**. In using her powerful testimony, she travels to reach people from all walks of life, from the unchurched, all the way to the leaders who are in need of healing themselves in an environment where they can "take off their masks." **Real Life-Real Issues** was birthed out of her home over ten years ago, and has now grown to be a cooperate fellowship that meets once a month to love on the lost. The heart she has for the abandoned, lost, and rejected comes from walking miles in those very shoes. Temecka has been in corporate America for twenty two years Due to the heart she has for people, she has found it hard to leave because of the amount of ministry opportunities that take place within the market place. Temecka and her husband, George, are the proud parents of four grown children, along with their five grandchildren, that keep their hearts full. They make their home in Knoxville, Tennessee. Her goal is to take God's truth to hurt people and show them how He can create beauty from ashes as he did with her own life. Temecka truly has a servant's heart and a trumpet set to her mouth to sound the alarm in this generation.

CONTACT INFORMATION

Email Address: Smitem444@gmail.com

SOCIAL MEDIA

Twitter:

Facebook Page: @Temecka Smith

Instagram: @Temecka Smith

GOD MAKE ME HER
Marcella D. Moore

Who can find a virtuous woman? for her price is far above rubies.

Proverbs 31:10

I first gave my heart to the Lord at the age of 17 at which time we only used the King James version of the Bible. Ninety-nine percent of the scriptures that I memorized today are from that version. Many years later technology and our love for education and the word exposed us to other translations of the Bible that provided a more in depth understanding. These translations, along with Holy Spirit, have opened my spirit to greater revelation and provided insight that empowered me as God's beloved daughter.

As gifted daughters in the church (we didn't use the word kingdom much back then), I along with my other girlfriends were encouraged to marry and not entertain long engagements. So at the age of 21 I became the wife of an amazing 22-year-old man of God. We were perfect for each other, our gifts flowed perfectly together and our love for God was reflected in our lifestyle. I was so happy to be married. We adhered to the scriptures (Hebrews 13:4), so we were destined to live happily ever after.

We were taught back then that our most important job was to take care of our husband and children. Like my husband, I worked full-time. I never pursued my dreams or took advantage of opportunities that I thought would out shine my husband. My job, as I accepted and loved, was actually to be a good and virtuous wife and mother. Being a good wife meant putting my husband's needs first, and this pleased God, so I was told.

I remember, often in my time of prayer at home and in church, thanking God for being a *virtuous* woman. I was growing into everything listed in Proverbs 31:10-31. I attended and spoke at conferences where the theme was "The Virtuous Woman." Those two words became a part of who I was, my husband and my children qualified me. As I became more in love with the different translations of the Bible, namely – New International Version, The Living Bible and New Living Translation to name a few, the word woman change to *wife*. The more I studied the more I embraced being a wife while not honoring the woman.

Fast forward to 16 years later after birthing 3 children (2 living), relocating to another state, purchasing a home and enjoying life, my marriage ended. I didn't understand because I served God and did everything I thought I was supposed to do. I took care of my family, paid my tithes and offerings, was active and went to church all of the time. I was very afraid because in my mind I was not capable of raising children alone. I never even imagined raising my children alone. I didn't know what it looked like. I grew up with both my parents and it felt great. My Mom was a housewife and my Dad was an amazing provider. So this definitely was not the life or outcome I signed up for, besides we both said that we loved God.

When I realized and accepted that my marriage was over (this took a very long time to accept), I felt lost like a naked person on a deserted island with a 10-year-old daughter on my right and 6-year-old son on my left. I didn't know who I was because all I knew to be was his wife – the virtuous wife who had abandoned the virtuous woman.

I've written about this time in my life often simply because it was one of the most challenging times of my life. Although my marriage officially ended in 2004 today I am still learning lessons from it. One of the biggest lessons I have learned is how important it is for us to know who we are as individuals. When we get married, we take on an identity as a wife and sometimes mother which both are only a small portion of who we are.

We put aside our likes and dislikes, we suppress the dreams and ideas we once had prior to getting married. We say yes when we want to say no because we want to keep our husbands happy. We feel guilty when we desire quiet time alone away from the family. We feel like loving who we are is selfish and not of God. I find that single women fall in this same category not with a husband but in their relationships and often times with their families because a stigma is placed on them as well. The pressure of not being married or having a child by a certain age; it's the same suppression of self. Before I continue, can we stop a moment so I can ask you some questions?

Who are you as an individual?

What do you like and love to do?

What makes you happy?

What is your purpose?

Why are you here?

These questions are so important. You must be able to answer them; in doing so, you get a better understanding of who you are. If you define your identity based on your marital, family or employment status, when those statuses change what are you left with? You must make time to define, embrace and celebrate yourself. If you don't you will look for people, mostly relationships to validate and define you.

The questions above are very important to answer but then there is another set of questions you must ask yourself as it pertains to your identity and that's your identity in God. As a daughter of the Most High God, you are created in His image and likeness. You are more than a conqueror, and if you obey Him you are everything and have everything and when you obey Him you are entitled to all of the blessings noted in Deuteronomy 28:1-14.

The pain and suffering I experienced through my separation and divorce was mostly due to the fact that I gave up myself, my identity, when I became a wife and mother. I automatically eliminated the virtuous "woman" and honored her as a virtuous "wife only." So when my ex-husband left, I felt that I was no longer a virtuous wife much less a virtuous woman. When he left he took the virtuous wife status with him, and I was left empty. I can't blame him for my emptiness, I choose to give up the woman because I thought it was the right then to do.

In order for you to successfully come through anything in life, you MUST know who you are. Self-discovery and self-development are very necessary, especially when you have lost yourself. God wants you to be your best God-self. He desires to know you, He wants to love on you, He wants a relationship with you, and He wants to reveal your true God self to you.

Unfortunately, as women, we often disqualify ourselves, forgetting that no matter our situation or circumstances we still belong to God. The different versions of the Bible as I mentioned earlier changes the woman in Proverbs 31:10 to wife, and we settle for that translation, believing we are no longer eligible to be that virtuous woman. Yes, this verse and the verses following mention husband and children who honor this woman of virtue but we fail to realize that before she became a wife and or a mother, she was a woman, a woman of influence, virtue and all of the other attributes listed in this chapter.

God wants to remind us ladies that our virtue, moral character, good heart, integrity and level of influence has everything to do with the person He has created us to be. It does not matter if you are single, married with no children, divorced or widowed; you are a virtuous woman. What makes you a virtuous woman? The fact that God created you in His image and likeness.

When my ex-husband told me he no longer wanted to be married, I thought my world was over. I felt as though I failed as a woman, wife and mother. I felt unworthy and could not see the light at the end of the tunnel. I cried every day, and I wanted to sleep my life away. It took me years to find myself again. What helped me was the love of my children. I know that some of you who are reading this may not have children, but I want you to know that you don't have to take years to find yourself or rediscover you again.

You must start by answering the question in Proverbs 31:10, "Who can find a virtuous woman," as noted in the King James version. The late Maya Angelou said, "We teach people how to treat us." If you carry yourself as a woman scorned, bitter, angry, bruised and hurt, who is not capable of carrying the virtue that God has placed on you, then people will see and treat you as such.

LOOK IN THE MIRROR AND ASK YOURSELF, "WHO CAN FIND A VIRTUOUS WOMAN?" (KING JAMES VERSION)

I want you to start by remembering. Remember your first encounter with God when you felt His love for you, and you knew that His love for you was unconditional and real. His love for you has not changed because of your circumstances.

Broken relationships and bad experiences often cause us to place God in the same category as the people who have walked away from you. He sees you as His baby girl, His beloved, His virtuous woman and the apple of His eye. He is not the church who has made you feel invaluable because of a divorce or the world who says that if you don't have a man you are not complete. He, Jehovah Jireh, the great provider completes you in every aspect of your life.

Let's read Proverbs 31:10-31

Proverbs 31:10-31 King James Version (KJV)

[10] Who can find a virtuous woman? for her price is far above rubies. [11] The heart of her husband doth safely trust in her, so that he shall have no need of spoil. [12] She will do him good and not evil all the days of her life. [13] She seeketh wool, and flax, and worketh willingly with her hands. [14] She is like the merchants' ships; she bringeth her food from afar. [15] She riseth also while it is yet night, and giveth meat to her household, and a portion to her maidens. [16] She considereth a field, and buyeth it: with the fruit of her hands she planteth a vineyard. [17] She girdeth her loins with strength, and strengtheneth her arms. [18] She perceiveth that her merchandise is good: her candle goeth not out by night. [19] She layeth her hands to the spindle, and her hands hold the distaff. [20] She stretcheth out her hand to the poor; yea, she reacheth forth

her hands to the needy. [21] She is not afraid of the snow for her household: for all her household are clothed with scarlet. [22] She maketh herself coverings of tapestry; her clothing is silk and purple. [23] Her husband is known in the gates, when he sitteth among the elders of the land. [24] She maketh fine linen, and selleth it; and delivereth girdles unto the merchant. [25] Strength and honour are her clothing; and she shall rejoice in time to come. [26] She openeth her mouth with wisdom; and in her tongue is the law of kindness. [27] She looketh well to the ways of her household, and eateth not the bread of idleness. [28] Her children arise up, and call her blessed; her husband also, and he praiseth her. [29] Many daughters have done virtuously, but thou excellest them all. [30] Favour is deceitful, and beauty is vain: but a woman that feareth the LORD, she shall be praised. [31] Give her of the fruit of her hands; and let her own works praise her in the gates.

God make me her! God has invested every attribute listed in these verses in you. Your job is to nurture, embrace and cultivate them and trust Him to fill the missing pieces. You may not have the husband or children that are referenced, but God as your husband can and will fill the void and allow the woman in you to be perfected thereby making room for the wife and mother to be manifested. Understand, if you never find yourself married or with children, you are still a virtuous woman. You still have everything that you need to be effective as a woman in this earth.

We as women in this world have been through a lot over the years. There was a time when we had no rights according to man. During slavery, we took care of our children, the masters children and all of the children in the community whose parents were sold or taken away, but God made sure that we were reminded that we had an amazing place here in the earth in the Bible. We are the giver of life, we carry, we birth, we are glue that, by God's grace, holds this world together. Our great Sisters of faith in the Bible include Sarah, Hannah, Abigail, Deborah and Jael just to name a few. We can learn from them and see how God allowed them to use their influence to be change agents in the earth. God make me her!

While I strongly encourage you to walk in your strength as a woman, I want to also remind you how influential you are in speaking life to men, empowering them and helping them rediscover their true identity. Discovering ourselves and knowing who we are does not mean belittling men or making them feel less than who they are. It does not mean that we take our independence and ability to stand alone to dismiss the fact that together men and women can do amazing things in God's kingdom. When we truly know who we are, we become better for our men, families, churches, communities, places of employment and the world. Knowing who we are, mixed with the influence God gave us as women, causes us to be effective and strong in the earth. Imagine if we take the same influence that Mother

Eve used in encouraging Adam to eat of the forbidden fruit, the changes we can and will make in the earth. God make me her!

If you find yourself in a church or ministry that does not encourage you to walk in the strength, power, wisdom and might that God has created you to walk in, you should strongly consider finding a place that causes you to thrive. Ask God to forgive you for limiting yourself and playing small and trust Him to lead you on a journey that will give Him the glory.

As you spend time with Him, getting close to Him, ask Him to show you Him so that you can see yourself the way He sees you. During your time of intimacy pray,

SUPPLICATION

Dear God, make me her! Forgive me for not seeing myself the way you see me. Despite my shortcomings, weaknesses and failures, make me her, the woman of virtue that will cause your light to be seen in all that I do. Make me her, give me the confidence I need to declare your word and wisdom in the earth. Make me her, allow me to be everything that you have called me to be so that I may fulfill my purpose. Amen

AFFIRMATION

I declare and decree that despite my marital status, I am a virtuous woman and every attribute of Proverbs 31 is manifested in my life. According to Isaiah 54, God is my husbandman, and He will not let me be ashamed. I stand on God's word - I am her and I am effective in every area of my life. God made me her!

APPLICATION

Ladies, I encourage you to connect with other ladies who can empower you and whom you can grow with. Please, if you have challenges with childhood trauma or domestic violence, make time to see a professional counselor or therapist. Asking for help is a reflection of courage and strength, asking for help does not make you weak. You have everything to gain by investing in yourself and nurturing your soul. Self love is not selfish; it's mandatory.

ABOUT THE AUTHOR

Marcella D. Moore, affectionately known as "Cella D", has been inspiring and empowering individuals for more than three decades. She is an Inspirational Speaker, Minister, Motivator, Mentor, Author, CEO, and Founder of Motivate and Pray, Inc. By means of tele-conferences and live events, she uplifts members of her audience with powerful words that inspire them to reach new heights.

Marcella is known to her audience as" the Reminder, Motivator and Life-Giver." She serves as an Ordained Elder at the Abundant Life Family Worship Church under the leadership of Bishop George and Pastor Mary Searight in New Brunswick, New Jersey. She facilitates the monthly Motivate and Pray empowerment and Caring for the Caregiver support calls. Both tele-conference calls serve as a resource for motivation, inspiration, empowerment, encouragement and prayer.

Marcella is also a four-time Amazon best-selling Co-Author. Her professional career includes more than 30 years in the corporate world as Manager, Director and Account Executive. Marcella volunteers with various organizations in the community. Some that are dear to heart includes domestic violence and teen mentoring. She is also a veteran of the United States Army.

She embraces her single-parent status and is the proud mother of her daughter Jessteni and son Elisha. Marcella's life journey has birthed a message in her that simply says, "Be a part of your own rescue, embrace your own journey, live on purpose and love yourself to life." Cella D's prayer is that the light of God on her life shines bright enough to make hearts open, babies leap and sleeping giants awake.

CONTACT INFORMATION

Email Address: info@marcelladmoore.com

Website: www.marcelladmoore.com

SOCIAL MEDIA

Twitter: celladmotivates

Facebook Page: celladmotivates

Instagram: celladmotivates

WHEN NIGHT FALLS
LaWanna Bradford

She perceives that her merchandise is good, and her lamp does not go out by night.
Proverbs 31:18

King Lemuel is cited once in the Bible. Though numerous speculations exists as to who he really was and where he reigned, these have been over shadowed by the words he used to describe in detail the qualities of a virtuous woman. As a reigning king, these were the characteristics that his mother urged him to weigh when selecting the ideal woman as his wife. This standard depicts a woman who is confidently aware that the product of her work is profitable, and her spiritual strength and resilience, as symbolic by the lamp, enables her to persevere through trouble times.

I identify with being in a heightened state of awareness and living a purpose-filled life. From an early age, I was always trying to connect the dots and see the relationship between things. I asked questions to fill in the blanks when my young mind could not make sense of my environment or the world. I remember my mother asking me why I always asked so many questions. Though I never said it, I often thought, "Why not ask?" As I look back, my life has been a never ending series of questions. Perhaps through these lanes of questions, I was led to my purpose. Like stepping stones, from experience to experience, I matured in my life's journey to where there was such a strong sense of knowing my "why."

When you can end your day and look on what you have completed and know that you have done your best in producing a quality product or service, you have the assurance that the profits will come. That is the lane that I was thriving in for over 10 years and all was well. I was living my passion of strategically guiding boards of directors and executive leadership of major corporations and government entities in key financial and growth decisions. I had arrived as a top 10% income earner in the U.S., and could see more opportunities opening up for me. Life was good.

I decided to leave corporate and take a little sabbatical before partnering with my brother in a residential mortgage business. That was a big leap from what I had been doing, but I was ready for the adventure of swimming in new waters. Life was even better than before. I was now doing things completely on my terms (so I thought), clients were flowing, our business was growing, and then the unimaginable happened. Nightfall hit.

"WEEPING MAY ENDURE FOR THE NIGHT, BUT JOY COMES IN THE MORNING"

– PSALM 30:5

If you have ever experienced nightfall where you wonder if you will ever again see the sun shining, you can empathize with my journey. Though my climb to what I felt was a life of overall success was gradual and consistent, the descent was rapid and painfully brutal. The economy hit a recession, my brother left the business, my marriage ended in divorce, and my business almost completely collapsed, and I exhausted almost all of my 401K all within an 18-month period. It was truly a dark period. For three years, I fought to get back on my feet and regain what I had lost. I struggled to do what I could to not close my doors as so many other mortgage companies and banks had done. I took several part-time gigs as a marketing consultant and as an English as a second language tutor. I even had to humble myself to call my parents to help fill in the financial deficit so I would not risk losing my home. Though I was crushed on every side, I was not broken, and I continued to press and trust and expect. God was a good God. That I never doubted, but I was beginning to question His mercy.

When I felt so weary with the struggle, I prayed for strength to not give up. Just as the virtuous woman whose lamp did not go out by night, the fuel in my lamp was God's word. I continued to recite His promises that He would never leave nor forsake me, He was my provider, and He the God of Faith was in my midst. It was through God's word, that I continued to press and hold on when everything that my physical body could see or feel was telling me to give up and call it a day. I would often question (here we are back to the questions) not why these things were happening, but what was I intended to learn from this nightfall. How could I turn what appeared to be stumbling blocks into stepping stones? Was there something I needed to do differently? What was God trying to tell me? What was the plan, since the original plan was derailed. These and a hundred other questions would race through my mind as I talked to God and waited for an answer. Days turned to weeks, and weeks to years (three to be exact) as I waited to see a light at the end of this dark tunnel. "God," I exclaimed, "You said weeping endures for night, but joy comes in the morning. Where is my morning, God? When will it come?"

The next day I received a call from a consulting firm asking me if I would be interested in interviewing for a senior management strategic planning position. They said it was only for three months, but I did not care. It was the opportunity that I had been waiting to come. I could feel it that this was different from all the other interviews that I had experienced, and it was. I was offered an amazing temporary position that turned into the highest paying position I had ever held, one which restored all that I had financially lost and gave me so much more over the years since saying yes to the offer. It had been a long journey, the night seemed to be never ending, but through God's grace and strength, my lamp may have flickered from time to time, but it never went out.

"MY LAMP MAY HAVE FLICKERED FROM TIME TO TIME, BUT IT NEVER WENT OUT."

Life in all of its undulating twists and turns brings us some amazing highs and some catastrophic lows, which I like to call tsunamic episodes. However, I have learned that we have been gifted with a beautiful life. When our purpose aligns with God, we can look at our work and see all is good. More importantly, when the winds blow, when the storms rage, and night falls, we can hold tightly to our faith in Him and know that our lamps will continue to shine for all to see.

SUPPLICATION

Heavenly Father, I want to thank you for loving and caring for me more than I care for myself. In this journey of life, you promised you would be with us always. Even when I lose sight or do not feel your presence, I know you are with me because I know your word is true. I pray you give me the strength to endure when life trails come my way. May I always look to you with a heart of thanksgiving when times are good or when they are hard. Let me not lose sight of you when the days are bright and sunny, or when the road gets a little rough.

I ask that you help me to hear your voice as I wait on you. You have promised, if I wait on you, you would renew my strength and that I would be able to rise with wings of eagles. You have taught me that in you I will be able to run and not grow weary and walk and not faint. Therefore, I pray I am obedient to your call. I pray I still myself and quiet my thoughts so I may hear your voice and follow as you lead.

I am facing a period of uncertainty and questioning, and I pray that you give me the right questions to ask and give me the patience to wait for the answers. It is a little dark right now and Father God I need you to shine a light on my path regarding _____*(State here what specific struggle or challenge you are facing that feels overwhelming)*. Give me the strength to stand and the courage to press forward in You. Let me not lose heart, but help me to sing you the highest Hallelujah praise knowing that you who have begun a good work in me are able to complete it. Remind me, when I grow weary, you are here with me. Help me to keep my lamp shining brightly. Though I may shed tears today, You promise me that joy comes in the morning. Bring the morning, dear God. In Jesus' Name I pray.

Amen

AFFIRMATIONS

I AM a child of God.

I know that God will never leave nor forsake me.

I AM able to do all things because God gives me strength.

I AM more than a conqueror.

I know that God is my supplier and my provider.

God is my very help in a time of trouble.

I know that my help comes from the Lord.

I am blessed.

APPLICATION

When Night Falls

It is much easier to stand on God's word and praise how good He is when life is going your way and everything is sweet. However, when the bitterness of life hits you, and you have done all that you can, that is when the challenge comes to hold fast to what you profess to know and to keep your lamp of hope and trust in Him shining. When the struggles come, these are the times when your confidence and faith in God must become that much stronger. It is during these moments of night fall when we must step aside and allow Him in all of his majesty to show His delivering hand to us. That is how we grow from glory to glory....from tragedy to victory.

When Night Falls Proclamation

Write a When Night Falls Proclamation that outlines what you will do in the Name of Jesus to keep your lamp shining brightly.

When night falls in my life, I will come against any thoughts of doubt and fear that may come my way. I will come against the spirits of worry, strife, and division. When night falls I will keep my lamp of hope and trust in God shining brightly by......

_____

_____

_____

_____

To overcome my doubts, fears, and worry, I will: (Solution)

_____

_____

_____

_____

Victory scripture. Write your victory scripture from the Word on which you can stand.

_____

_____

_____

_____

Who can you use as a resource to stand in prayer with you and be a source of encouragement?

_____

_____

ABOUT THE AUTHOR

LaWanna Bradford is a serial entrepreneur and global leader in the strategic planning and performance management arena. She is a thought leader and business management consultant who applies strategic thinking and business management concepts to maximize efficiency and effectiveness, and identify both business and life opportunities for improvement and growth. She is the COO of The Bradford Group, a commercial and investment mortgage brokerage and the principal of The Bradford Group Consulting, a business management consulting firm. As a change agent, she leverages her 30+ years of experience working with federal and private industries and small businesses to guide individuals toward achieving growth, understanding their market position, and increasing awareness of the customers they serve. LaWanna is certified in Strategic Planning and Quality Management and Georgia Oglethorpe Board Examiner's Training. She holds a Bachelor of Arts in Sociology from the University of Arizona, and a graduate degree in Administrative Organization and Management from Golden Gate University Graduate School of Public Administration. Her passion for shifting paradigms that allow women to elevate to the highest versions of themselves is magnified in the Celebrate You Women Embracing Wellness & Life movement that she co-founded. LaWanna is an international best-selling author, public speaker, trainer, philanthropist, artist, avid reader, and writer who loves nature and spending time with her family. She believes life should be embraced in the moment of now and positive transformation and lasting impact in life and in business is achieved one strategy at a time.

CONTACT INFORMATION

Email Address: lawanna@bradfordgroupmtg.com

Website: www.bradfordgroupmtg.com

SOCIAL MEDIA

Twitter: @LaWannaBradford

Facebook Page: @lawanna.bradford.3

LinkedIn: lawannabradford

HOW TO FLOURISH IN FORGIVENESS WHEN HURT BY GOD'S ANOINTED?

Jacqueline Goodwin

"She riseth also while it is yet night" "Proverbs 31:15a
"her candle goeth not out by night." Proverbs 31:18a

Wisdom is needed when dealing with hurt. However, God gave me some additional tools to assist with forgiving his anointed which was praying and fasting. These tools became the avenue for me to flourish in forgiveness. Often, when we are hurt it makes us to become stagnated because bitterness takes root. Praying and fasting will uproot unforgiveness and bitterness.

The Proverbs woman rises at night it is during the night that God can really speak to us because we have settled in from our busy day. At night we become a watchman for the souls. It was during the night that God would have me to really intercede on behalf of God's anointed. Praying keeps us in constant communication with God so we will follow His will and not our own. Communication is key in prayer, because if we do not talk with God we will never learn the heart of God. Praying allowed me to forgive all of the pain that God's anointed caused me. It pushed me into a position of totally yielding to God.

Proverbs 31:18a gave me the pictured of the Proverbs woman fasting on behalf of her family and community. Fasting is a tool that will keep us alert and our light never going dull. Fasting provides us with clarity and making sure it is God's voice we are hearing and not our voice or other voices. God began to show me that my hurt must be dealt with by fasting and praying. He took me to Matthew 17:21, "Howbeit this kind goeth not out but by prayer and fasting." As I sought God to break the bondage of pain caused by his anointed, he led me to fast three days out of the week going without food and drink. Falling to resentment, facing bitterness and fighting hate my only

117

help was fasting and praying. It amazes me how betrayal can resurrect so many emotions and feelings at one time. As I begin my fast, I would ask God to search my heart and purify my thoughts. It was during this time He revealed to me that the pain was only dormant but needed to be evicted. He led me to read Isaiah 58:6, "Is not this the fast that I have chosen? To lose the bands of wickedness, to undo the heavy burdens, and to let the oppressed go free, and that ye break every yoke?" The pain caused by God's anointed became a heavy burden for me. It was a yoke upon my neck that only fasting and praying could break. Though I was a woman of God His chosen vessel I still struggle with my pain. One thing I have learned about the pain it does not matter what title you carry in ministry it will take resident in your life, but how long it dwells there depends on us.

How could I allow somebody else to cause me to fall into a state of resentment? Easily, because I did not address the pain that was caused like so many of us do today. Women, we place bandages and patches over our wounds, never allowing the hurts to heal. I resented the fact that God even allowed me and the pastor to cross paths. The more I wondered why he came into my life the more resentful I became. I begin to understand that my pain was not going away but growing into animosity and hostility. We must get control over our pain because if we refuse to control and confront it, we may forfeit our destiny. Also, not having control or confronting our pain produces negative thoughts in our minds about God's anointed who hurt us which can lead us into becoming a woman God did not create us to be. When I started having negative thoughts and becoming a woman who God did not create me to be, it was then I knew that this was bigger than me and only God could heal me. I begin hating myself for allowing God's anointed into my inner circle. I hated the fact that I was not in control of my pain, yet I still had to preach, prophesy, and pray, and teach Sunday school. I was miserable. I asked God how He could allow me to be hurt by His anointed. God opened my eyes to this revelation that though one may be anointed, he is still susceptible to causing pain. The only exception of His anointed that did not cause pain was His son Jesus Christ.

Fasting and praying were tools that started my breaking down the wall I had built, and these tools removed the delay to my total healing. However, through this process, I gained a nugget from God. In my time of prayer, God revealed to me that the most painful situation can be transformed by bringing it to Him in prayer It was Satan's plan and desire for me to remain in prison, but I realized that pain is prison and freedom is forgiveness! God delivered me out of prison and when He did, He brought me out with this eye-opener: forgiveness brings forth transformation. Though God's anointed have hurt you apply these steps as they will assist you in your healing process, helping you to empty your mind and heart of anger, bitterness, resentment; replacing both with love and forgiveness towards God's anointed. As you allow God to heal you during these stages, your mind and heart will be transformed with forgiveness, and you shall reap the benefits of God-exalting you and promoting you into a newness in Him that you have never experienced. Once your heart and mind have been transformed and free from the pain, you will be able to see God's anointing on your life. He provides you with new opportunities. You will discover underneath your pain lies your destiny!

The pain had stolen my life and purpose, but being obedient to the steps God gave me pushed me into my destiny. Though your mind may have been comprised with unforgiveness and brokenness, you're healing is evidence that your pain did not destroy you nor hinder you. It only pushed you to victory! Forgiveness is action. It is something you must do, and by praying and fasting, you will find peace, healing, and deliverance.

The only antidote to unforgiveness is praying and fasting. As Jesus asked His Heavenly Father to forgive those who crucified him, those who brutalized him, those who trampled over Him, He was transforming. He was no longer bound to His physical body, but He elevated to His spiritual body. There on the cross, a change took place before His elevation. Therefore, if do not allow your healing to take place you will never possess what is new! I encourage you to embrace your pain because it is a steppingstone to a journey of healing! Let us close and seal our healing with prayer.

SUPPLICATION

Heavenly Father, today I come to you asking for your guidance to lead me to the type of fast that you would have me to participate in to bring forth my healing . Lord, my time of fasting and praying allowed my eyes to discover the purpose you have for me beneath my pain as you promised to me according to Jeremiah 29:11, "For I know the thoughts that I think toward you, saith the Lord, thoughts of peace, and not of evil, to give you an expected end." Even though I do not understand the purpose of my pain this very moment, I trust you, Lord, to make it clear according to your Word in Luke 8:17, "For nothing is secret that shall not be made manifest; neither anything hid, that shall not be known and come abroad." Lord, I want to be made whole. Therefore, I surrender my all to you so that your healing virtue will make me whole. And I thank you. For even in my pain, I know it is working for my good. I seal this prayer with the blood of Jesus and in His name! Amen!

AFFIRMATION

Recite these affirmations daily!

I will forgive God's anointed so that I will be forgiven. Luke 6:37

My fasting shall bring forth my deliverance from all bitterness, wrath, anger, and clamor! Ephesians 4:31.

My praying shall sustained me because I have cast my burdens on God! Psalm 55:22.

My praying and fasting shall free me from all pain because I now walk where the Spirit of the Lord is. 2 Corinthians 3:17.

APPLICATION

1. Realizing that you are not superwoman, but you are a woman who is suffering from a wound. Praying/fasting peels off the layers of your hurt helping you to recognize how your hurt has kept you in bondage and spiritually paralyzed you.

2. Fast:

   a. Have a clear purpose for your fast (inner healing, forgiveness towards God's anointed, include his name in the fast).

   b. Decide the length of the fast.

   c. Decide the type of fast (Daniel 1:8-14 {from certain types of food}, Esther 4:15-16 & Acts 9:9{Full fast}, Sexual { 1 Corinthians 7: 3-6}).

3. Pray:

   a. Ask God to help you heal.

   b. Ask God to help you forgive him.

   c. Ask God to reveal godly counsel for you to confide in

4. Meditate on God's Word: (healing Scriptures)

   a. Psalm 147:3

   b. Psalm 142:7

5. Journal what God's word revealed to you regarding your healing during your time of fasting/praying.

ABOUT THE AUTHOR

Jacqueline Goodwin is an ordained pastor and prophetess whose ministry focus is deliverance and healing. She has a passion and heart for the youth which has led her to various positions within the ministry and career field. Since 2002, Goodwin has served as Youth Director, a mentor, and Sunday School teacher within her local church. A former paralegal, educator, and substance abuse counselor who used her gift of empowerment to transform lives within her career field. She has earned a Master of Arts in Practical Theology from Regent University, Master of Counseling from Webster University, Columbia SC, a Master of Pastoral Counseling from Liberty University, Lynchburg VA, an Associate Degree of Paralegal graduating "Magna Cum Laude" from South University and a Bachelor of Arts in English from Francis Marion University, Florence SC.

She currently resides in South Carolina with her son, two daughters and granddaughter. Her hobbies include running, walking, meditating, and writing, counseling youth and working in the community.

CONTACT INFORMATION

Email Address: Jacquelinegoodwin0507@gmail.com

Website: www.healinginthevesselministries.com

SOCIAL MEDIA

Twitter: @Jacquel58497682

Facebook Page: @lenisegoodwin

Instagram: @lenisegoodwin

IS YOUR MERE EXISTENCE ENOUGH?

Sebrena Sumrah-Kelly

To everything there is a season, and a time to every purpose under the heaven. ~
Ecclesiates 3:1

One's purpose in life is the very meaning of existence. Without this present, we shall succumb to distraction, failure, and regrets. We will surely suffer from ignorance denying ourselves this. Many will fall prey to propaganda that life contributions do not matter and thus the world ought not to see one's, the impact that could be. I know now that there is always purpose in all of God's children and living with a mission to serve. I discovered that we all have a season, and when that time forces its way to be revealed, we have to receive the assignment and become obedient. No woman or man was created to fail or be a liability, but rather a vessel to serve the unjust, voiceless and underprivileged. I also know it takes confidence, but we must never forget God already gave us that, so trust we must focus on what we are capable of. Greatness is within all of us, but too many times self-doubt emerges along with the people around us that confirms the false beliefs. The desires are within us all, but too many times our circumstances intervene, and as I said, placed on a shelf for many years.

Why was PURPOSE Absent!

For many of us, we have no idea or daily thought of ones' purpose. Merely existing and surviving day to day is what most of us know. Many of our upbringings were simply to enjoy the life presented to us, complete school and head onto college and then comes a family, no mention of purpose along the way. Women, as we know, are the foundation of family, our first nurturers.

What is the concept of "life's Purpose?" No one really promoted or emphasized PURPOSE, especially early in life. Purpose is usually omitted in daily conversations. I do believe many of us were numb to purpose. We might have wanted it but was not sure how to get it. Many faced daily challenges of turmoil, where survival was a priority, thus there was no room to crave purpose.

Life has a way of just passing day by day.

Mothers go all in for family and neglect themselves. Days become years and a light bulb appears, what happened to me. No one bothered to ask!! No one had a reason to ask!! No one said congratulations!! I allowed that precious thing called time to ROB me of ME!! The beautiful thing about life is remaining vigilant!! It always waits with no complaints. It craves attention so the world can witness what it already knows. Yet we continue to dismiss the very being that is you. We allow distractions to dominate and stifle a gift from God, yours. My goal is to allow you to and grant yourself permission to Rediscover that which lies hidden. We all have an audience!!

Emergence of PURPOSE

I don't recall hearing the word PURPOSE growing up in Guyana, South America, No discussion with Mom, teachers, friends, church… If I did, it did not resonate. Upon migrating to the United States of America, we moved to Brooklyn, New York in 1985 with my Mother Linda Smith (a single parent). I began another chapter of my life in a foreign place, a new culture, a new school, new friends. I heard, "Stay in school, graduate, and you will get a good job with excellent benefits."

I discovered it upon migrating to Atlanta GA, in 2002, in my mid thirties'. I was a single mother coming to a town with no job and no place of my own. A fresh start with no contacts, no direction, only change for a new life after divorce. With my precious baby girl, Amani, dreams of becoming someone in Atlanta (a place where I read "it's the place where BLACKS are progressing). PURPOSE then showed up. I wanted how to embrace and start the new journey. It took work, dedication, strength, courage, more importantly, my LOUD VOICE. I only knew how to be a mother to my daughter, seek employment and provide a comfortable life.

YES, QUITE A BIT OF YEARS I LOST, BUT AS WE KNOW, GOD'S PLAN NEVER CEASED, IT REMAINS AWAKE FOR YOU MY SISTERS.

Where does Purpose fit in this? Purpose emerges and you suddenly realize it laid dormant, inactive, stagnant. As I look back at my birth, childhood, school years, marriage and a mother, there was no thought of my PURPOSE. Yes, there were quite a bit of years lost, but as we know, GOD's plan never ceased, it remains awake for YOU my sisters.

After hearing an advertisement on one of Atlanta's prominent radio stations for a networking event, I heard business, connections, meeting people is what one will experience at the event. It got my attention. I lived in Stone Mountain, GA, (With my mother's friend, leasing a room in her home). I heard Stone Mountain, GA as the city announced!! (Is it Faith), I think so. I remembered still not working (but the event was FREE), so I knew that I had no excuse not to attend.

With no instructions on how to dress or what to expect I was about to attend my first networking event. Coming from a corporate world, I knew how to dress in that world, so my business suit was a must. I do recall I needed a touch up for my hair, but I made it work. Purse in hand and off I went. The most profound moment at that event was when I was asked to present my business cards. I replied that I did not have one or a business. I clearly remember a woman that greeted the guests. She said to me, "Girl you better get a business." I went home feeling empty that I had nothing to offer and no one knew I was there, no one knew I existed, and a sadness came over me (that although I was a mother, I am grateful to be alive and place that was not my own. I did not have anything to share with those people.... I had no voice, nothing at all to contribute. (I vividly remember that feeling as I share my story with you now). You might be feeling the same way, that you have no sense of purpose, because that is what it was; we just did not know what to call it.

How to embrace Purpose (It's going to take work):

Each day, we grow mentally and spiritually. As we know it, life begins to reveal in bigger forms. We begin to see life and time differently. As the curtains close and the kids are put to bed, we are alone and GOD, the same GOD whom you did not know, was always there begins to speak louder and louder... "Wake up, you have work to do. I did not create a bystander, nut a NOISE MAKER and you will not Remain Quiet."

I've learned that time is not REFUNDED, once it's gone, it will never come back. But your mere existence is TIME to say YES to Purpose. We all have our own audience, and guess who is the MAIN Attraction, YOU!!!

Purpose will never rest, get weary, or retire!! It drives you to exceed exponentially. The more you act, the more it will get clearer. Many will find that you will sometimes get in your own way, and so will others. I say, that is a testimony that you will soon tell an audience just like you are reading my words today. A whole new you will have to be reborn and Trust in GOD.

For I know the plans I have for you, declares the LORD, plans to prosper you not to harm you, plans to give you hope and future.

You must know that your dreams are yours to dwell in every day of your life. Some days it may seem quite challenging, but those days are to be embraced and celebrated.

God's creation of Women transcends race, culture, and background. It's that "BIG" my sisters, to include YOU. Do not pay attention to the constant chatter that you are "NOT" or incapable of!! You are to be appreciated and thus your "VOICE" must be loud, and your purpose must remain vigilant. You are not the title given by man but by your creator.

Single Mothers: You are his gift; you are not by accident. You are here to serve and were placed in this unique place to overcome. You will cry but will smile at the strength you will have to possess.

Wives: You are his gift; you've created a sacred foundation.

Mothers: You are his gift. You are a nurturer and yet you remain unselfish.

Independent Woman: You are his gift. You are not defined by anyone.

Grand Mothers: You are his gift, and you remind us of the shoulders on which we all stand. You have taken the brunt, yet we ask how. You have taken us under your wings and showed us all how to FINISH WELL.

GOD CALL ALL WOMEN, WE ALL HAVE AN ASSIGNMENT: DON'T IGNORE THAT CALL.

Know the Phenomenal Woman that you are and ROAR with no apologies.

Women keep flying; you have wings, use them.

Dear sisters, we've all heard that we have a unique calling, purpose, a path only assigned for you. Well, it is true!! Think about it, upon birth that is the beginning of that assignment. The clock starts to tick, and life as we will see it shall be!! You will begin life's work.

Although we are not responsible for the environment in which we are born, we are responsible for our own individual lives. We all have our own paths, which will reveal the purpose as you will learn. We will dream about it, although it may not come true for a very long time, we must keep dreaming. We were not created to simply go along day to day and exist with no real plan or purpose. I urge you (if you are reading this and life is just stagnant), it is not the final call. If changing your demographics, changing your job, changing a spouse, changing your vocabulary is what has to be done (**then you have WORK to do**). I lacked an environment that fed me purpose. Yet in my 30's I found purpose. As a young girl, in my village growing up, my primary school, secondary school, even high school, as I migrated to America, stood out (my grades/report card). "Sebrena TALKED too much," my teachers would say. I can smile now, although it got me into trouble with my grandma and my teachers (**it is who I am today**). I simply will not shut up!! WHY, because I found my **VOICE,** which is now a part of my legacy. I remind my daughter so many times to speak up even to the ones she adores and admires. I urge you to remove FEAR from your life; it will STIFFLE YOU. It will stop you from that experience you see others get to enjoy, LIFE'S ASSIGNMENT.

You have heard the saying: "Don't get in your own way." Well, it is true for us all. Remember, purpose is yours, and it benefits and enriches the lives of others. Some will say it also has a monetary incentive, but we've seen where that is not the case. Many stories of prominent individuals who rose to what we believe the highest form of success and yet (fulfillment, purpose is lacking), some have relinquished all the wealth and fame for that thing called PURPOSE.

SUPPLICATION

I humbly come to you; I trust you in all my decisions. You are my salvation. Please continue to use me as you see fit. I know what my purpose is and that is to SPEAK to the voiceless and give them their own VOICES. I am thankful for you creating me. I know that the weapon of DECEIT and distrust shall not prosper in my life. I thank you for protecting me from all that have launched towards me with malice. I choose to take a stand and humble myself and not retaliate against my enemies, Lord. For your strength that runs through me is enough to conquer. I declare that my enemies shall not prevail but will bend on their knees to worship you. You will lay hands on them as they seek redemption. In Jesus Christ, to whom I praise. Amen.

AFFIRMATION

I shall continue to claim victory in all that I am and all that I do.
I will reach many more with the sound of my VOICE.
I am a woman who shall continue to give.
I will remain faithful even in times of uncertainty.
I am a woman of integrity.
I promise to be kind and remain humble to all that come before me and around me.
I will not abandon myself.
I am a servant leader.
I will find people who want more.
I love myself.
I will be selfish with me.
I will have abundance in everything I do.

I will not live a life full of regrets.
I will look FEAR in the eyes and Prevail.
I will talk to God in challenging times.
I will remain obedient even when fear seems to be the easy way.

APPLICATION

Take a stand Proclamation:

Wherever you go, go with all your heart, PREVAIL you must.

Do not allow others to influence you. Listen to your saviour; listen to your heart (they are always on your side). Your life partner is your saviour. Limited beliefs will prevent you from getting what is rightfully yours. I am taking a STAND for my savior, Jesus Christ. I often stand in my own way, I often doubt myself, and I often Delay and procrastinate. You must make the decision to be unstoppable which creates abundance in your life. So shall my word be that goes out from my mouth; it shall not return to me empty, but it shall accomplish that which I purposed, and shall succeed in the thing for which I sent it.

I am taking a stand: To overcome my challenges: I will listen more to my savior and shut out the noise that seems to consume me that serves me no Good. Please forgive me for all the times I have hurt others. Help me forgive those that hurt me. I will do better with your grace.

To overcome my challenges, I will: be bold and develop a posture like no other, one that will protect me and keep me driven. I will no longer be affected by criticism and stop caring what people think. Eliminate competition. **Honor her for all that her hands have done, and let her works bring her praise at the city gate. Proverbs: 31:31.**

Sisters, remember to feed your purpose daily with only what will uplift you, the Holy Bible, empowerment words and daily inspirational vitamin. This foundation should be daily subscription

We all have a bigger calling, sometimes it is not always revealed to us when we ask, but it will come when it is ready to be.

ABOUT THE AUTHOR

Sebrena Sumrah-Kelly, A Native of Guyana, South America, is the Founder and President of the Caribbean and American Global Business Connections and The Global Sister Who Speaks. She is known as the Global Connector. She is an International Keynote speaker.

Sebrena, is a global TV & Radio hostess & Producer, Ambassador, Motivational Speaker, Actress, and Business Coach. She is a master Networker & Mentor and has leadership platforms in over 35 countries with several franchise partners in the Network Marketing Industry and the Travel and Tourism Arena.

Sebrena mentors and empowers communities locally and globally, to remain committed to their purpose and entrepreneurial gifts.

Sebrena, has been featured in Countless Publications such as: Who's Who in Black Atlanta and the People You Need to Know Magazine presented her the Woman of the year Trailblazer Award. Atlanta's prominent publication Rolling Out Magazine, nominated Sebrena Sumrah-Kelly as one of the top 25 women to know and do business with in Atlanta in 2013. In 2018, The Voyage Atlanta Magazine featured Mrs. Kelly, highlighting her contributions to the City of Atlanta in entrepreneurship and media.

Resolution No. 1699 was presented to Sebrena, by the US House of Representatives in the state of Georgia for her Global efforts serving communities. In 2020, Sebrena Sumrah-Kelly, will be launching her Global Women Platform for Women who are the unsung voices of their communities. She reminds her audience to SERVE the VOICELESS. The global sister platform will speak of her nationality, her truth, and her love for communities. Helping a sister one by one, she will be The Global Sister Who Speaks.

CONTACT INFORMATION

Email Address: SebrenaSpeaks@gmail.com

SOCIAL MEDIA

Facebook Page: @SebrenaSumrahKelly

Instagram: @sebrenaspeaks

UNDER CONSTRUCTION
Dr. Derashay Zorn

She girds herself with strength, And strengthens her arms.

Proverbs 31:17

When I think about Proverbs 31:17, I imagine something being renovated with a portion of it under construction while the other portion is available for use. In the portion of the property that is suitable for use, people are still able to work or live in that portion because is usable space. On the other hand, the area that is under construction, only those who are authorized can come into that zone. Nothing from that zone that's under construction affects the area that has already been develop and good for living or working. I believe that this standard operational procedure is something that the Proverbs 31 Woman operated in her life and should be adopted by all believers. It doesn't matter what title we hold or how many degrees we have, there is always a place within us that is under construction.

Wherever something is under construction, there is some kind of development taking place. However, while what's being develop is progressing as needed, we can still function in the work that we are called to do. King David knew areas in his life had to go under construction when he wrote Psalms 51 and stated, "Create in me a clean heart and renew a steadfast spirit in me. His didn't abandon his position as king, but he humbled himself under God so that he could fix King David's issues. Right there, as he reigned as king, God was healing him. As areas of his life went under construction, we do not find this place affecting any other areas of his life or him continuing in the things that exposed his weakened areas. In addition, when the work was done all things was new, and the King never acted on it again. As I think of the woman described in this verse, I think of a women under construction and renovation is consistently at hand as she utilize what's accessible and develops what's required. .

When we look at the Proverbs 31 Woman's attributes, one would think she had it all together from the start. However, under close observation, we will discover that she was in a consistent place of developing herself. This was a woman who was very assured of her strength and understood there was opportunities for her to grow and develop. In spite of her short comings, she didn't use them as excuses to slack or operate from a place of insecurities. Instead, she eliminated and relied on her areas of strengths to look flawless in her assignments.

Wherever she showed up her strength took center stage and made her shine. While in the background, she was cultivating and making the necessary adjustments so that she can show up the next day even better than she did the day before. Even though she didn't have it all together, you didn't have to worry about her bleeding while leading. This woman did not put others down to cover up her flaws so that she could feel good about herself. She didn't try to overcompensate to make up for her areas of improvement. She wore her crown very well. She must have had an understanding that she was fearfully and wonderfully made. The woman knew how to show up and not allow her flaws to get in her way.

A virtuous woman gird herself with strength so that she may be prepared for her journey. Proverbs 31:17, would give us the indication that this woman had vision. Not only did she understand that she had a purpose, but she was on a mission to bring her vision to past. This woman was very goal oriented and intentional about everything she did.

As I focus in on this text I am learning that this woman is giving all she has while bettering herself. I believe that a Proverbs 31 Woman accesses her current location against her destination and determine what it was going to take to get her there. In terms, she begin to set goals to achieve what's necessary so she could arrive to her destination with nothing missing or lacking. Then once she beat that goal she didn't get stagnated, she reached for the next destination on the journey. The Proverbs 31 Woman was very strategic in how she operated. The woman didn't take on every task at one time, but she did her task one at a time so that her work would not go uncompleted..

The words girds applies that she prepared herself with the resources she had to complete her tasks. She didn't allow what she didn't have to distract her from the task at hand. This woman knew how to manage what she had so that she would see the manifestation of her expected end.

USE WHAT YOU HAVE AND USE IT TO GET WHERE YOU NEED TO GO!!

- DR. DERASHAY ZORN

There is a valuable lesson to be learned from this woman. She shows us that we have more then enough in resources to begin the work of the Lord. Therefore, we should never be hindered in moving forward in our God given assignment.

134

The Proverbs 31 Woman didn't compare herself to other and how they operate. This evidence is in the fact that she looked within herself to gather what she needed to advance in her assignment. Many people are not moving forward because we are to busy watching the resources of others. During the observation of others, we find ourselves forming limiting beliefs and minimizing our abilities of completing the task. As a Proverbs 31 Woman, we cannot compare ourselves with others. We must understand we all are tailormade by God and what one may need for their journey another may not. Because we are uniquely designed by the hand of God, we have everything necessary to move in purpose. Along the way, we will be equip with what's necessary to grow in purpose.

When a house is build its put together one brick at a time until the foundation is but in place. Then in its appropriate timing, they bring in the other components to finish building the house such as the pipes, electrical wiring, drywalls, etc. I believe that is how we walk out our purpose. We have what's necessary to get started, and God will provided the additional resources at its suitable time. The word says be faithful over a few things and He will make you ruler over much. This woman was faithful over a few things as she girded herself with strength. Therefore God put even more in her hand.

A Proverbs 31 Woman doesn't rely on other people or things to give her strength or value. She finds it within what God has given her. When we depend on other things or people to strengthen us, we are placed in a vulnerable position and it hinders our progression in the purpose that God has for our lives. When we feel the need to have something or somebody to complete us for the journey, we become stagnant and complacent when we don't have these things. It makes us feel insecure, inadequate and cause us to never start or stop moving in the things that God has called in our lives.

When our dependency is on things and others, it is like the house that is built on quick sand. When the storms, trials, rain, come you quickly fall apart due to a foundation that didn't have the compacity to hold you up. Our dependency must be built on that which is solid and can hold up when the storm comes. Jesus Christ is the rock and the foundation in which we should depend and stand upon. Dependency on anyone other than Christ will cause us to fail. To complete our purpose we must be God dependent and nothing else. Therefore, look at what you have, know that's it's enough to get started, make the best of it, rely on Christ to strengthen you, and utilize it to advance into the promise of God.

This woman was not ignorant neither did she ignore the fact that development was necessary to complete her purpose. Therefore, she strengthens her arms. She knew she had enough to get started but understood that what she had was not enough to complete the fullness of her journey. This is the place where she closely observed her purpose, acquired and needed resources, current position and condition, then mapped out the best course or action to develop what she had and acquire what she need. It requires humility and strength to honestly examine yourself and take a course of action for improvements. The word tells us that we are transformed from one degree of glory to another in 2 Corinthians 3:16. This means that we should be strengthening our arms through some form of growth and development. If we don't develop we will die, therefore, strengthen your arms so that you may grow and prosper.

> **IF WE DON'T DEVELOP WE WILL DIE. THEREFORE, STRENTHEN YOUR ARMS SO THAT YOU MAY GROW AND PROSPER.**
>
> - DR. DERASHAY ZORN

If growth and development was necessary in this walk then Christ wouldn't have ask God to send us the Holy Spirit. So that He can teach us all things and bring things to our remembrance.

I remember waking up one day to an awaking within me. This day was not my ordinary day. I usually rise to the same old song of emptiness with unfilled dreams that I just knew was out of my reach. I'm not sure what took place that caused me to arise with a different song. I wanted something different, and I knew that the usual was not going to get me there. I had to go under construction so that I could gain the strength for a journey that my limited belief doubted that it was possible. As I overserved myself in the most vulnerable position ever, it begin to terrify me. I was in a place of total dependency without nothing to support me, if the one who I depended on decided that he wanted to leave. I couldn't have done anything to quickly recover.

The vulnerability of being 21 years old, with three children, only completing the 8th grade, and a stay at home mom was not a place that I ever envisioned myself. I could purchase food, clothes, or anything for myself or my children from anything that I had of my own. Now I must give God the praise that it wasn't an environment like King Pharaoh of Egypt operated. There was no lack and financial abuse wasn't present, but it was room for it to happen. As anxiety began to rise, I dreaded the unfavorable possibilities of my situation. I believed the Lord began to quicken my spirit and bring back into my remembrance my dreams and goals of old. I wanted to finish high school and college, get married, become a computer programmer analyst technician, have children, buy a nice house in a good neighborhood, have a nice car, be wealthy, be able to take care of my grandma, and live happily ever after. I wanted the generational curse to be broken so that my children wouldn't be a part of the vicious cycle that help my family back from pursuing our dreams.

At this point I had to make a decision to either stay in the vulnerable position that I was in or gird myself with strength and strengthen my arms. It was time for me to believe in my dreams and goals. I understood that if I didn't make the right decision that my boys was going to be caught in the generational curse. Therefore, I grew in my relationship with God so He could lead and guide me. As I persuaded my dreams and desires, what made me successful in my personal, professional, and educational endeavors was that I took the internal and external resources God had given me and utilized them efficiently. As areas in my life under went construction, I utilize what was available for use to advance.

What I didn't know that God was preparing and positioning us for what was ahead. We didn't know years later my boyfriend, who became my husband, would be fired from his job of 16 years and his income would no longer be available to support us. Had I not girded myself with strength and strengthen my arms, we would not have been prepared for this tragedy. I would not have the education level needed or work experience required to obtain my newly given position at the college that would support our household independently for a few years. This job lay off gave my husband the opportunity to gird up his strength and strengthen his arms as he pursued education for a career change. He didn't have to worry about the household because the day of my awakening put me in a state of alert to prepare for the worse. It turned out that it was for the best as I took action on pursuing what I always desired.

I encourage you to take an examination to access where you are and compare it to the places of your dreams and desires. Then put in place the road map that would lead you to your destination. Capitalize on your strengths and allow them to be utilized to their full potential. Put an under construction sign in the zones of areas of weakness and threats, and allow the appropriate authority, King Jesus, in so He can fix it.

SUPPLICATION

Dear God,

I thank you for creating me in your image and likeness. It is my desire that I begin to operate as you have designed me. Therefore, I come upon your throne humble as I am ready to go under construction. I ask that you examine me, and whatever you find that's not of you, do the work that is necessary to make me whole again. In this life, I have encounter many things that has hindered me from being true to myself and going after the dreams you have placed in me. Teach me, Oh Lord, how to strengthen myself so that I may prevail over my adversaries. In this day, God, I request that you train my hand of preparedness so that I will always be ready for the task ahead. As I thank you and know that I can do all things through Christ that strengthens

137

me as I cultivate and develop in the truth of your words. In Jesus name, I ask these things, Amen, Amen, and Amen.

AFFRIRMATION

I am faithful over what's been given to me.
I am a steward over my resources.
I am very strategic.
I have more than enough to get started on my purpose.
I can do all things through Christ that strengthens me.
I will not compete or compare myself with others
I will rely on Christ alone.

APPLICATION

<u>STRENGTHEN YOUR ARMS</u>

To strengthen your arms, you must place a goal before you so that you can have a target to aim your endeavors.

<u>Goal:</u> What is your expected end?

<u>Plan of Action:</u> How do you plan to get there?

<u>Access Your Resources:</u> What internal and external resources do you have or will need to accomplish your goal?

<u>Remove spots of vulnerability</u>: Review your list of current resources and examine to see if you have become dependent upon them. Develop strategies to remove areas of vulnerability in your life, even if it's your own self. Don't forget to list areas where you lack trust in God. Develop a plan of what you would do if the resource was not there. How would you make it happen. Find scripture in the word of God to help strengthen you. Then start executing the plan.

<u>Go under construction:</u> Review your listed of needed resources and locate the areas in your life that need cultivating so that you can strengthen your arms. If you need to develop your relationship with God, enroll in school, hire a coach, see a Christian counselor, partner with another organization, etc. don't be afraid to do it.

<u>Light up the world:</u> As your arms are strengthened show off and put to use the great work that God has done in you.

ABOUT THE AUTHOR

Kingdom Strategist, Blueprint Builder, and Spiritual Midwife, **Dr. Derashay Zorn** is an international business coach and expert in the art of **unleashing purpose, developing dreams, and expanding untapped potentials within individuals, corporations, and ministries.** Her passion for information technology has led her to obtain a Master of Science in Information System Management which equipped her to **specialize in analyzing, developing and managing systems to birth or expand individuals and entities into the next dimension of kingdom implementation.**

Derashay equips mankind globally as the Founder of the **Kingdom Influencers Network, In The Church™ TV & Radio Broadcast, Divine Order Restoration Ministries (D.O.R.M) International, Kingdom Strategist Firm, Women of Influence Magazine, (D.O.R.M) Publishing** and many other entrepreneurship endeavors that equip mankind globally. Through, her global brands **Kingdom Strategies University® & School of Authorpreneur®,** she teaches others **how to maximize their potential and monetize their gifts and talents** as a critical vehicle for fulfilling their purpose, making a significant impact and branding influence that can instantly and beautifully change the world. Her books and workbook titled **"Abortions In the Church: Divine Strategies to Spiritual Deliverance" & Meant for My Good: Being Developed In The Midst of the Disaster** is helping others overcome and give birth to their purpose, visions, and dreams. She is a wife, mother, pastor, entrepreneur; consultant, empowerment speaker, mentor, and friend.

Her philosophy is **"A critical tool for self-development is learning how to cultivate, build and release others into their destinies."**

CONTACT INFORMATION

Email Address: info@derashayzorn.com

Website: www.derashayzorn.com

SOCIAL MEDIA

Twitter: @kbstrategist

Facebook Page:: @kingdombusinessstrategist

Instagram:: @kingdomstrategist

ABOUT MY FATHER'S BUSINESS

Dr. Tranell Steward

Jeremiah 29:11 (NIV)

11For I know the plans I have for you," declares the LORD, plans to prosper you and not to harm you, plans to give you hope and a future."

2. Timothy 1:7 (ESV)

7 For God gave us a spirit not of fear but of power and love and self-control.

S ince the beginning of time, we as women have had to overcome so many obstacles, whether inside the four walls of the church, our homes, or on our jobs. There are arguments made even now that discourage women from speaking up, informing their truth, or leading as God has called many of us to do. Much of this comes from our experiences, religious ideologies and cultural boundaries that create environments in which women choose to remain silent. How then can we really expect to lead, let alone have any influence as an entrepreneur?

I am a minister, I am a wife, I am a mother, and I am a entrepreneur with multiple degrees under my belt, yet I still considered myself unqualified to lead. A trait that is necessary in order to step out into a field that, until recently, was dominated by males. I used to wake up every morning, like many of you, trying to understand my purpose, still learning who I am, weak at times, struggling a substantial amount of the time, and broken; yet God called me to do and be something that many would not make it easy for me to be. God called me for a specific purpose and despite what I would go through, that purpose didn't change. I had to change. It took some time to understand that God did not call me because I was qualified, but he qualified me before the call in order to fulfill that purpose. That purpose was much bigger than me, something I would have to depend on him to accomplish. It wasn't about what I had the ability to do myself; it was about my willingness to submit to his will for my life.

Your destiny is set. You were purposed even before the breath entered your body. God knew you before you were formed in your mamma's belly. His plan for you is not based on the mistakes you made, the experiences you have had, or what people have said about you; it's based on your purpose.

What I love about Jesus is he would always surprise us with his ways, leaving many of his followers and religious scholars stunned at times, specifically this intentional care for the women he made contact with while he walked in his flesh suit. One thing that many of the women of this day had in common, was that they were broken, humiliated, ostracized, yet determined. I want to bring attention to two of the women that helped me to understand how loved I am, the value that I hold, and what was required of me as a woman on assignment.

The Woman at the Well

This account is found in John 4, after Jesus sat alone, exhausted from his journey with the disciples. He had a chance encounter with a woman at the well. It's worth noting that the scholars report this conversation Jesus has with this woman as one of the longest conversations he has had with anyone, even his disciples. I suggest it took a lot to convince her of who she was despite the way she had been living.

Jesus was having a conversation with a Samaritan, a despised race, a woman whose people even looked down upon her . She was marked as immoral, an unmarried woman living openly with the sixth in a series of men. This woman is outcast and she expects nothing but what she is used to getting from the world. She has accepted what they said about her, and she let her past, and in this case, her current lifestyle, keep her quiet and feeling undeserving. It was her that continued to question his care for her because of how she was living. She could not see any value in herself or purpose in her life. Jesus, despite her, loved her through this conversation by encouraging her to change her ways, giving her a promise of grace and forgiveness.

God will speak to us from a place of victory not one of shame. Often times we are hiding from God, when he is in full pursuit of you in order to prepare you for what he has for you. We hide from God when we know we are not living a life that is pleasing to him. I spent years running from him for this very reason.

In my youth, I was challenged. My identity was defined by my experiences. I made decisions as a young girl that would shape me as a woman. It would shape my mindset about who I was and what I was worth. Let me tell you, I was very similar to the woman Jesus met at the well. It would take what seemed to be a lifetime to reshape those thoughts I had to define me as a woman. The same thoughts that prevented me from believing I had purpose, that my life meant something, and that I was here on assignment. I fought with where he was calling me because I didn't feel worthy.

The Woman with the Alabaster Oil

The day that I heard about this sinful woman that shows up in at the house of the pharisee, where Jesus is having dinner, I could absolutely relate to her. As I read in Luke 7, I was very clear, that when she showed up that day, she is on a mission. Let's look at what happens starting at verse 6

⁶ Now when Jesus was at Bethany in the house of Simon the leper, ⁷ a woman came up to him with an alabaster flask of very expensive ointment, and she poured it on his head as he reclined at the table. ⁸ And when the disciples saw it, they were indignant, saying, "Why this waste? ⁹ For this could have been sold for a large sum and given to the poor." ¹⁰ But Jesus, aware of this, said to them, "Why do you trouble the woman? For she has done a beautiful thing to me. ¹¹ For you always have the poor with you, but you will not always have me. ¹² In pouring this ointment on my body, she has done it to prepare me for burial. ¹³ Truly, I say to you, wherever this gospel is proclaimed in the whole world, what she has done will also be told in memory of her."

The problem the disciples had with this was not only that this oil was expensive and it seemed to be a waste of value, it was that the woman pouring it was not worthy to be in the presence of Jesus. Though it was not clear to the disciples why this woman was spilling this expensive oil on Jesus, this action was filled with purpose. She was a sinner that was put in position to effect change because of her desperation to be cleansed by him.

What stood out to me about this woman and her encounter with Jesus was that she was so desperate and full of so much faith that she refused to ask permission. When we are desperate enough we will take action. When you been through enough hell you will crave change and you will go after it with everything you have. Sometimes it takes us to hit rock bottom to really get this desperate. But it's this kind of desperation that moves us out of our comfort zones. This is the place where God can truly move and direct freely. I learned so much from these unnamed women and their encounters with Jesus. Both of these stories gave me something that a college education, nor my experiences could give me. It helped to reveal my purpose.

I cannot talk about being a successful entrepreneur without getting to the root. The success for anything you choose to do is based on where you are plugged in, where you get your source of power from. These two women were unnamed, I believe for a reason. God wanted us to put our focus on the action presented in each story, showing us what it would take to achieve success. We see here how much God values us and longs to give us the desires of our heart. However, the levels of success he wants to give you cannot be accomplished without him.

There is a saying that goes, "If you want to make God laugh, tell him your plans." We can't get access to those plans without having this intimate time with him. This is especially needed before you make any decisions on opening a business or becoming an entrepreneur. The scripture says, for I know the plans I have for you. It doesn't say you choose, you go out there and do it in your own strength. Why wouldn't God send us out in that way? It's because the thing he has put on the inside of you is too big for you to handle on your own. Eyes have not seen, ears have not heard kind of blessings are what we should be investing in.

I joke often with my friends that God loves to tease us. He will show us the end result, but never give us the steps in between. There are reasons for this. If we knew what it took to get to his promise, most of us wouldn't go. We worry so much about what others are doing and the steps they are taking in order to make sense of the promise, but I guarantee if God gave it to you, it's not something you would obtain easily by just looking at someone else's journey. If we could, then what would we need God for. He wants your time because there are certain things that cannot be deposited until you do just that.

There has been plenty of times that God has shown me something or told me to go do something, and I refused because I didn't have the right attitude about it. I didn't understand why he wanted to use me; I didn't recognize what he said about me when I looked in the mirror. I had every excuse as to why I was unqualified, and it made sense. I just needed to convince God of that. However, just like the woman at the well, God saw what I was unable to see in myself. He was able to speak truth to me because he knew what he had deposited in me. My relentless attitude to be the best leader or entrepreneur I can be comes from knowing that in spite of me, God has a purpose on my life, and that purpose is designed to impact every person I come in contact with. Find your purpose, and you will not have to seek success; it will find you.

SUPPLICATION

Father, I thank you in the name of Jesus, for giving me a purpose and trusting me with it. I thank you lord that despite my past, regardless of how much I hurt you, you still came after me. You are my power source. No other source will I plug into. Teach me to seek you in all my ways. I will forever acknowledge you and be at peace with your leading. For I know that the _____ (business, calling, assignment) I carry is yours to do with what you will. I am a willing vessel. I know I cannot accomplish a thing without you giving me the steps in between, so I dedicate all that I do unto you and I will intentionally seek you to get the tools necessary to accomplish your will for my life. Let the words that I am praying today take up residence in me as a reminder to seek you first. In Jesus' mighty and precious name I pray. Amen.

AFFIRMATIONS

1.   My service is a gift to this world, and I will share it.

2.   I am building a company that will make an impact daily.

3.   My work makes a difference in this world.

4.   I am a smart, successful, woman of God.

5.   The success of other women entrepreneurs fuels me with energy and joy.

6.   Whatever I can dream up for my business, I can achieve.

7.   I create daily opportunities for growth for myself and others.

8.   My failures have made me a better entrepreneur.

9.   My income is growing every day by doing something I love.

10.   The passion I have for my work enables me to create real value.

11.   There are no limits to what I can achieve.

12.   I am driven by passion and purpose.

APPLICATION

Decide today that you will no longer do business as usual. I had to learn this truth the hard way. I want to save you the heartache and pain of starting something that was never meant for you to do something that was never in your heart. Be intentional in your pursuit of purpose from God.

Prepare the following statements and post them on the places you frequently visit (EX: work desk, bathroom, bedroom mirror). The word says write the vision and make it plain. Once you write these statements down, they will help you stay the course.

My Why? _____ (Why are you doing this? what is driving you?)

My Vision? _____ (What has God revealed to you....)

My Mission? _____ (How will you get there...)

Read these statements out loud daily.

ABOUT THE AUTHOR

Tranell Steward is a serial entrepreneur with a passion for developing and growing nonprofit organizations and businesses that serve with purpose; having the ultimate goal of securing successful leadership in businesses that serve youth and young adults across multiple industries. She sees this as her opportunity to help organizations reach their potential and become 'organizationally-actualized'. She has a very diverse and extensive educational background with a Bachelors in Criminal Justice, a Master's in Business Administration specializing in Leadership Development and Marketing, and is a Doctoral Candidate in the field of Behavioral Science with a focus on Human Services. Her work in building connections from nonprofit organizations and ministries that serve at risk youth to the sports and entertainment industries has afforded her the opportunity of receiving an Honorary Doctorate in Transpersonal Psychology. Tranell Steward is the Owner and Senior Management Consultant for U1st Management Enterprises LLC, a management company that serves entertainment professionals with a unique purpose to enact change through their work, consulting with entrepreneurs and industry professionals in order to help them effectively initiate and carry out their strategically devised plans of action. She utilizes many different platforms in order to educate and inspire purposeful change organizations and businesses.

CONTACT INFORMATION

Email Address: consultdrt@gmail.com

SOCIAL MEDIA

Twitter: Dr. Tranell Steward (@TranellDr)

Facebook Page: @DrTranellSteward

Instagram: @DrTranellSteward

MY SECRET TO HAPPINESS
Wakeitha Cunningham

Then he said to them, "The harvest is great, but the laborers are few; therefore, pray the Lord of the harvest to send out laborers into His harvest. Go your way; behold I send you out as lambs among wolves."
Luke 10:2 - 3

The Gospel of Luke portrays Jesus as an equipping Leader. He focuses on the teaching ministry of Jesus, that He equips and empowers every hungry person who comes to Him. Those that came to Him full and satisfied got nothing; however, those that came to Him starving received everything needed. This book teaches us that healthy leaders have nothing to prove, nothing to lose, and nothing to hide. Luke teaches us that the most powerful force in a leader's life is LOVE for the people. Luke portrays Jesus as a perfect Man that lived a perfect life of leadership and authority. Everywhere Jesus went, he led. Everywhere Jesus went, he served. The Gospel of Luke introduces us to stories of generosity through men and women, both mature and immature in their faith and shares how they participated in normal activities and still managed to live abundant, generous lives.

The Called Giver, not by choice but through the request of Jesus. At a young age I remember learning the values of reaping and sowing. Through my grandmother's love of giving, doing for and sharing with others, these values and lessons were instilled in me. My grandmother is loved by many in her community, church and family. Growing up, I remember always wanting to be loved like that! Like so many others, I can say I had a childhood that wasn't the best, but looking back over my life I can truly say that through it all I Thank God for all that he brought me through and for giving me the life he did, which has made me the person I am today! As a child, there were parts of my life I wished could be different during those specific periods of time, and I remember times when I enjoyed certain periods of my childhood. Like a lot of families, our family was not perfect, and we had our share of challenges. I remember dealing with family members that were alcoholics, drug addicts, those that had violent tendencies, compulsive cursers, mean, negative, lack of education, and so many other issues kept us separated from Jesus Christ. No matter what was going on during that time, I always felt that I was different. I somehow knew I was not supposed to be that way, and I truly believed God had a purpose for my life, but I just didn't know what it was. I remember thinking, "I'm going to do all I can to figure that out" because I didn't want to be like them. In Luke, Jesus sent out over 80 of his early disciples to give up everything and go out into the harvest, to share the good news and to help people with their needs. These disciples were called to go out and take nothing, not a dime, no clothes, not even a snack to support Jesus out of their means but at times by giving all they had! My actions through childhood and as I've gotten older aligns with that of The Called Giver.

It was hard to operate in who God called me to be because I struggled internally with the question "Who am I?" I did not know how to define my identity. For a long time, I did not know my purpose, and I really didn't know how to figure it out! Honestly, I found myself taking on the identity of who people wanted me to be. I was in and out of church throughout my teenage and early adult years till it came to the point where going to church was just routine. I didn't have a relationship with Jesus Christ. I was just going religiously because I was taught that was what we were supposed to do! I think that routine got boring to me, so I eventually stopped going because I figured I was wasting my time. After that, I picked up other habits, some good and some bad that led me to do things that were definitely out of character for me. I knew some of the things I was doing were not who I was either. During this period of trying to find myself or figure out my true identity, I began getting more involved in the extracurricular activities that my children were involved in. I was alright with it because, to me, I was doing something I thought made me happy! The older my children got I found myself still doing more and more of the things they enjoyed within their environment. I became more and more content with my happiness being dependent on something going on for someone else rather than myself. In the midst of it, I didn't realize doing and giving to others was my true identity. Since it wasn't something I thought was a gift or purpose for my life as my relationship with Jesus got stronger, I started learning more about who I really was and my true purpose! The Book of Ephesians teaches that God provides church members with positions of authority, then provides them with gifts and positions. Paul follows God's lead by equipping the people to use their gifts in service. He instructs others to find their calling and pursue it. Here is where the question was answered, and I stopped finding my identity in how people saw me and started thinking about my identity in how God sees me. I was being taught to see the new identity given to a person

150

when they were in Christ.

In Ephesians 1:1-14, we are reminded of our positions in Christ: chosen, predestined, accepted, redeemed, informed, heirs, and sealed. Paul declares what God has done for us before demanding we do anything for Him. Since God has done so much for us, it is our duty to serve and give to others out of love for Him. Once my understanding of being a called giver was realized, I began to understand more of the traits I had that I never understood before. In Exodus 36:1-7, we see God's people bringing more than enough to meet the needs of others, giving more than was asked to give of me was something that I found myself having to eventually set boundaries

GENEROSITY:

A CANDLE LOSES NOTHING BY LIGHTING ANOTHER ONE.

HELEN KELLER

on. Although I was **chosen** to give to meet the needs of God's people, my purpose was not to hinder them but to equip them to use their gift to meet their needs. During this time in my life, I felt I was being used and taken advantage of leading me to question my purpose again and have a second thought about what I was called to do. However, my spiritual growth led me to give a response to what I thought was great causes. Here is where I think I was **predestined** to serve and give in the field of women's empowerment and give more than money and resources but give my time, knowledge and my gifts, which proved to be better utilized. Similar to the story in 2 Corinthians 8-9, I started giving faithfully to help a community of people, some that I met and some that I didn't meet. As a called giver, my gifts, whether large or small, taught me the importance of sacrifices. Volunteering and serving when there were no monetary gain involved was and still is something that did not bother me, and it was something that was actually rewarding to me. I enjoyed being able to give and help people in ways that filled me with joy and happiness, and in return, pleased God by doing what he called me to do. I realized that God had equipped me with more than just money to give; he'd given me influence and a heart to teach and empower others to find and use their gifts for the good of others. While using my gift to empower other women and/or families that were going through different situations, I was growing in my own faith and learning to trust God with the little bit I had, not expecting anything in return. I felt I had reached a point in my relationship with Christ where I really felt accepted for using my gifts, and I thought as though I was being redeemed in God's eyes for turning my back on him as an immature Christian. During this time, I remember my Pastor preaching about having faith in what God says in the word instead of believing what man says about us.

That is when I decided to step out on faith, so my faith grew stronger, and I knew if I stayed in his word and trusted him, he would provide for me and give me what was needed to help other. Also, during this time I remember my Pastor teaching on using the gifts we had been given and explaining that our gifts were not for us but for others and was for God to get the glory for. Something that also stuck with me during this time was Pastor B's favorite scripture Roman 8:28 – "And we know that in all things God works for the good of those who love him, who have been called according to his purpose." Then is when I remember learning that change happens from the inside out, and if we want to think like God, we must renew our minds and preserve our bodies to Him as living sacrifices. We must also trust him to revolutionize our lives and transform them as only he can.

On my journey to H.O.P.E, I can honestly say that I had to do a lot of soul searching and faith building within me. I sometimes question my gifts and the reasons God chose me to be how I am, but one thing I have learned on this journey is that I lead by my own values, beliefs and convictions. I give and lead with passion and substance and I connect with both the head and the heart in every decision I make. Since God is holding me responsible for how I lead his people, my goal is to motivate through grace and relationship, not guilt and religious rituals. Like God, I work to change people from the inside out, not the outside in.

EACH OF YOU
SHOULD USE
WHATEVER GIFT YOU
HAVE RECEIVED TO
SERVE OTHERS, AS
FAITHFUL STEWARDS
OF GOD'S GRACE IN
ITS VARIOUS FORMS .

1 PETER 4:10

SUPPLICATION:

God, I thank you for saving me and allowing me to work with you to share your joy with others. Help me not take for granted the gifts you've given me. Lord, help me to have eyes to see the needs around me and to respond to those needs with hope and joy. God, continue using me to be the change you want to see in this world. God, continue directing me by lighting my path and giving me directions for where you want me to go. God convict me when I am purposely rejecting what I know you are sending me to do. Please continue giving me the strength to be put out there so I can "Let my light shine before others." For Lord, I know that a lamp's light is meant to be placed on a stand to give light to the people around it. God, condition my heart and hide my flesh in the midst of what you're doing in me and through me so people will see you in me, and You will get all of the glory and recognition. Because I am not perfect and may struggle with the sin of _____ (list a sin that you know you need to repent of and ask for forgiveness for), I ask for your forgiveness, and I ask that you help me take a look at my own life and work on changing my heart in those areas before I can expect to help others. God, help me not be conformed to this world, give me the words to say so my words are used for good and not bad. Help me consider the company I keep, the places I go and how I use my influences. Lord, help me to make choices where I'm considering other people's needs to help them meet their needs and not hinder or criticize them. Help me to give people the benefit of the doubt and be patient with those I'm called to serve or help. Most of all, Lord, I ask you to continue holding me accountable for treating other people the way You want them to be treated. God, I Love you and I thank you. I pray all these things in Jesus Christ name. Amen.

AFFIRMATION:

I am a giver. I am a warm, giving person.

Everything I give to others is a gift to myself. As I give, I receive.

I am giving and compassionate.

I give freely without expecting a reward.

The best way to find yourself, is to lose yourself in the service of others.

I am extroverted, friendly, giving and helpful.

The more wealth I receive the more I will have to give and share.

I give and receive freely.

APPLICATION

What are Your Secrets to Happiness?

A quote from Booker T. Washington states, "Those who are happiest are those who do the most for others." I believe this to be true because through my doing for others is where I find joy and happiness. In 2 Corinthians 9:6-7 – the point is this: "Whoever sows sparingly will also reap sparingly, and whoever sows bountifully will also reap bountifully. Each one must give as he has decided in his heart, not reluctantly or under compulsion, for God loves a cheerful giver." Therefore, you are not only serving others when you do for others you are serving God, and you will reap what you sow.

Write a My Journey to H.O.P.E. (Happiness on Purpose Everyday) Goal. Every day you should write down one thing you can do intentionally to be happy on purpose. Is it showing gratitude for what God has given you? Is it performing an act of kindness? Is it calling a friend or family member to mend a broken relationship?

What one thing can I do to make me happy and feel good about myself? (Action)

_____

_____

To reach this goal, I will (perform the action, give specific details).

_____

_____

Write what you did and how it made you feel.

_____

_____

Write down your H.O.P.E. goal and action plan for the next day.

_____

_____

154

ABOUT THE AUTHOR

Wakeitha Cunningham is a Certified Life Coach and Personal Finance Coach, who is passionate about helping women live with happiness, meaning and purpose in both their personal and professional life. She helps professional women identify barriers which have kept them stuck by helping them create a life success plan, so they can pursue their God-given purpose.

Her heart to serve others led to her position as the L.I.F.E. Program Coordinator for the Family Promise of Hall County, a non-profit organization that provides shelter and assistance to displaced families. Wakeitha enjoys volunteering and empowering women. When she is not serving others, you can find her spending time with her children, reading, traveling, networking, and attending self-development training. Coach Wakeitha Cunningham is an Influential Woman of God who is intentional and passionate about living her life with H.O.P.E (Happiness on Purpose Everyday).

She contributes her drive and success to being a mother of two. Wakeitha graduated from the University of North Georgia with an Associate of Arts Degree in Social Work. At a young age Wakeitha was taught the Golden Rule of Life, which was the importance of doing unto others as you would like done unto you. Wakeitha has always had a heart for helping and empowering people. Wakeitha is a true believer in the verse Acts 20:35: "It is more blessed to give than to receive." She believes her purpose in life is to help others by inspiring, encouraging, motivating, empowering and serving them however she can. Wakeitha is on a mission to touch the lives of God's people one at a time by encouraging them to have H.O.P.E ~ Happiness on Purpose Everyday!

CONTACT INFORMATION

Email Address: info@wakeithacunningham.com

Website: wakeithacunningham.com

SOCIAL MEDIA

Facebook Page: @coachwcunningham

Instagram: @coachwcunningham

CONSIDER THE COST

LaWanna Bradford

She considers a field and buys it, and from her
profits plants a vineyard.
Proverbs 31:16

The virtuous woman, as described by King Lemuel, is a woman with admirable and morale qualities befitting of a wife of a king. One of these many attributes, with which many women today struggle, is the art of negotiation and money mastery. During the patriarchal time of King Lemuel, men held the primary power and predominate roles in political leadership, moral authority, social privilege and the control of property. However under Jewish law, women had the right to own land without a man representing them. If a man died without having sons, his inheritance would pass to his daughter. This leniency in the law created an opportunity where women could develop financial literacy associated with owning and managing of land and finances.

In this passage, a woman is engaged in negotiating two complex transactions. She is buying a plot of land and then from her merchandise profits, she plants a vineyard. This is a classic example of leveraging money to acquire an item which will in turn produce more money. This Proverbs woman demonstrates that she is wise enough to not invest her money in a depreciating asset but rather in one that will grow in value over time. She also allowed the produce of the land to serve as a second income stream for her. If you contemplate this a bit more, there could have possibly been a tertiary source of income resulting from this business decision --- the pressing of the grapes into wine, perhaps.

When the contemporary woman reviews all the traits of a virtuous woman, it can be very discouraging if one compares their life to that of this imaginary woman. This priceless individual, who appears to be able to do everything and still have time for herself, is an idealist reflection of the perfect woman as told to King Lemuel by his mother. God is not seeking perfection from us. Through his love and mercy-we are able to daily serve God and proclaim his goodness in our lives. This is how we grow from glory to glory.

As a serial entrepreneur and investor, I have been at the negotiating table many times as both the buyer and the seller. About 20 years ago, I ventured out and purchased my first investment property. It was a single-family bungalow built in 1924. It was perfect with its beautiful French doors, two fireplaces, and a fenced backyard that even had a dog house. I wanted to make my money work for me, and I thought it would be best to renovate the home, rent it out as a long-term rental and generate cash-flow.

Since I had a mortgage loan for the property, I used money from my savings to begin the improvements needed on the home. What I failed to consider were hidden repair items that are inherent with renovation projects. One by one they showed themselves, from the sagging and warped flooring, to water damage under the crawl space, mold remediation, and the list kept growing. If any of you have ever seen the movie with Tom Hanks called *The Money Pit*, you know exactly what I was facing. I even had the hole in the floor that was depicted in the movie.

With each new "need to get it fixed" item, I had to become a quick study to understand what the contractors were telling me so that I would not be taken advantage of during this "cosmetic" process. I soon became quite fluent in the language of home renovation and found my rate of errors and money lost growing less and less. Finally, after several contractor terminations, and approximately twenty thousand dollars more in repairs than I had first projected, the home was complete. At that point, my new husband did not want to have anything to do with the property. He said he was tired of seeing the stress of the deal, even though he had nothing to do with it nor had he invested anything in it. He demanded that I sell it rather than try to rent it. To keep the peace in my home, I took what was intended to be a long-term investment and another retirement stream, and put it on the market.

I hoped it would be a fast sale, but it was not. It was a buyer's market and even with the savvy skills of my realtor, the bungalow sat and sat without even a nibble of interest. So I added some cosmetic touches to the home to try to entice a buyer. I had a few calls of interest, but that came with attempts to negotiate a lower sales price, which I could not afford to do since I needed to get my money back out of the house. At this point, I just wanted to break even, and taking a loss was not an option.

Unfortunately, the longer it sat and spring rolled around, the street began to bustle with a level of activity that I did not foresee. When I purchased the bungalow, it was during the winter where there was only an occasional walker down the street. The real activity, the true pulse of this community was hidden from view as people hibernated indoors. With the warming of the air, spring became the welcoming call for the drug addicts and prostitutes. Now,

I had another problem. How was my realtor going to sell the house because we never knew if someone would be camped out on the front patio or coming up out of the crawl space where they had been conducting some illegal drug or sexual activity on my property. I felt so violated and was at a loss of what to do. I could continue to call the police to come out and get the trespassers off of my property, but within 24 hours they or another crew would be back squatting as though it was their own. Though I was thankful that the windows and inside was never vandalized, the exterior air conditioning units were harvested for their copper and they continued to find a way into the "secret lair" that the crawl space provided.

I journeyed down the road and thought of creative and strategic tactics to protect my home. I decided to have a conversation with a local prostitute who I often saw walking up and down the street. I will never forget her face. She was so thin from the drugs that her dresses hung on her such that she was always fumbling trying to pull up a shoulder strap that would find itself falling down low and exposing what she tried to publically conceal, yet privately revealed. It was her face that spoke to me. She had a wide broken tooth smile and the deepest dimples. Her dark eyes, which had seen so much pain and loss, seemed to twinkle a bit whenever she saw me wave at her.

One day, I decided to ask her if she would watch the house for me. I knew this was an invitation for trouble, but I thought since she was always on the street she probably knew everyone. I asked her to just keep the drugs off my property and the people out of my crawl space, and I would pay her $50 per week for helping me out. Well, she did just that. I have no idea what she said to the people, but whenever I would drive by-they were not on the property.

Finally by late April, I was elated when my realtor called to tell me that we had a cash buyer. I breathed a sigh of relief when I heard the offer because though I did not make any money on the property, I did not lose any either.

> "DO NOT JUDGE, OR YOU TOO WILL BE JUDGED. FOR IN THE SAME WAY YOU JUDGE OTHERS, YOU WILL BE JUDGED, AND WITH THE MEASURE YOU USE, IT WILL BE MEASURED TO YOU.
>
> – MATTHEW 7:1-2

There are times when I think back to that first investment transaction and the prostitute who kept an eye out for me. I wonder what happened to her. I want to believe that she found a better life off the streets. My little bungalow, however, is one of those financial decisions that if I could rewind the clock, I would not sell. I have to admit, I do go through the *should've, could've, would've* scenarios in my mind. I sold what I had invested for my future. At the end of the day, the marriage I was hoping to keep together in a state of peace became tumultuous and eventually ended in divorce.

All in all, it was a hard lesson of disciplining myself to make decisions based on counting the costs and artfully negotiating even with the one you love. I believe a win-win is possible when two sit at the table and truly listen, and hear the other side. This is a life lesson that has served me well as I find myself always assessing opportunities and strategically negotiating for that win-win that allows me to be at peace when I close my eyes.

> **"I BELIEVE A WIN-WIN IS POSSIBLE WHEN TWO SIT AT A TABLE, AND TRULY LISTEN AND HEAR THE OTHER SIDE."**

Lessons to Consider

When entering into negotiations, there are three steps that the Proverbs woman did. She considered, she bought and then she planted (i.e., invested). Let me take you through each of these.

Consider a Purchase – When you are making a purchase, assess what you are getting and then negotiate the terms and conditions that you want. It is important to count the cost before you move forward in a decision.

Buy It – After weighing the cost and assessing the risks, then make the purchase. Set an intention for why you are doing something and step away from those emotional buys and be deliberate in your decisions. Calculate the yield or return that you want to have, which does not always have to be a monetary return, and then make a wise decision.

Invest – This is a critical step that so many miss. We find ourselves purchasing things that have a diminishing return, but we do not take the time to consider how it might bring added value by working for us. This means that when you purchase something and it is truly an appreciating asset, this is something that when planted into will bring forth good fruit and monetary blessings. This is an example of looking for ways to make money and investments work for you. Just like the Proverbs woman who planted a vineyard using her profits.. This produced vineyard grapes she could sell and perhaps even have a second business selling wines

SUPPLICATION

Heavenly Father, I want to thank you for being my Jehovah Jireh, my provider. Thank you for your Word which reminds me to bind wisdom and knowledge about my neck. Thank you for ordering my steps and for the Holy Spirit who is my Comforter and Guide.

I ask that you help me to remember to be patient when making decisions. Let me take a stand and not allow anyone to rush me into making decisions that are not according to your perfect timing and order for my life. Show me the path so that I may see the increase that has been laid out for me, and for the purpose that you have called me at this appointed time in my life.

I have often made many decisions without counting the cost. I have been guilty of allowing my emotions to drive what I do, and I do not want to be a slave to my emotions. I pray that I am liberated by the power of the blood of Jesus Christ. May I walk boldly and proclaim dominion on the handiwork of my hands and the labor of my heart. Bless me indeed, Lord, and enlarge my territory.

Father God, I have a critical decision to make, and it requires that I speak with someone so that they understand my side concerning _____*(State here what specific thing you need to make a buying decision or just any decision that requires you to be able to exercise your negotiating skills)*. I pray that we reach a win-win and that I am able to walk away knowing that a good and perfect work and outcome has been done and will manifest. I pray that I be patient and that I temper my tongue. May the words of my mouth and the meditation of my heart be acceptable in your sight, dear Lord. Help me to be quick to hear and slow to speak as I seek to understand the other side before I make my request.

I thank you that your banner over me is love and that all things are possible through Christ Jesus who strengthens me. In Jesus' Name, I pray and expect the manifestation of the win-win. Amen.

AFFIRMATIONS

I AM a child of God.
I love all mankind.
The Lord is my light and my salvation who shall I fear.
My steps are ordered by the Lord.
I am quick to hear and slow to speak.
The light of Christ shines brightly in me.

APPLICATION

Consider the Cost

Haste makes waste is an old adage from Benjamin Franklin, but he was not the originator of the idea to pause and consider the cost. God's Word tells us to not begin until we have counted the cost. It causes us to ask the question why would we begin constructing a building without first calculating the cost to see if there is enough money. This applies to all things that we do, especially when we are making purchases and are involved in business decisions. Do we count the cost, or do we go after the short-term gain, but fail to look at the long-term impact? Is the cost of our time, talents and money evaluated when we invest them and the return that we may get from them?

Consider the Cost Proclamation

Write a Consider the Cost Proclamation that outlines what you will do in the Name of Jesus to ensure that you are cognizant about considering the costs before making major purchases or business decisions.

When I find myself needing to make a major financial purchase, or I need to be involved in making a business decision, I will

_____

_____

_____

To become a better steward over my financial household and the increase that God has blessed me with, I will: (Solution)

_____

_____

_____

Victory scripture. Write your victory scripture from the Word on which you can stand.

_____

_____

_____

Who can you use as a resource to stand in prayer with you and be a source of accountability?

_____

_____

ABOUT THE AUTHOR

LaWanna Bradford is a serial entrepreneur and global leader in the strategic planning and performance management arena. She is a thought leader and business management consultant who applies strategic thinking and business management concepts to maximize efficiency and effectiveness, and identify both business and life opportunities for improvement and growth. She is the COO of The Bradford Group, a commercial and investment mortgage brokerage and The Principal of The Bradford Group Consulting, a business management consulting firm. As a change agent, she leverages her 30+ years of experience working with federal and private industries and small businesses to guide individuals toward achieving growth, understanding their market position, and increasing awareness of the customers they serve. LaWanna is a certified in Strategic Planning and Quality Management and Georgia Oglethorpe Board Examiner's Training. She holds a Bachelor of Arts in Sociology from the University of Arizona, and a graduate degree in Administrative Organization and Management from Golden Gate University Graduate School of Public Administration. Her passion for shifting paradigms that allow women to elevate to the highest versions of themselves is magnified in the Celebrate You Women Embracing Wellness & Life movement that she co-founded. LaWanna is an international best-selling author, public speaker, trainer, philanthropist, artist, avid reader, and writer who loves nature and spending time with her family. She believes life should be embraced in the moment of now and that positive transformation and lasting impact in life and in business is achieved one strategy at a time.

CONTACT INFORMATION

Email Address: lawanna@bradfordgroupmtg.com

Website: www.bradfordgroupmtg.com

SOCIAL MEDIA

Twitter: @ LaWannaBradford

Facebook Page: @lawanna.bradford.3

LinkedIn: lawannabradford

KINGDOM VALUE

Carissa Brown

---

*For you formed my inward parts; you knitted me together in my mother's womb. I praise you, for I am fearfully and wonderfully made. Wonderful are your works; my soul knows it very well. **Psalms 139:13-14***

The Webster's dictionary defines value as "holding something in high regard; determine how much something is worth." In the Bible, there are several scriptures and parables that bring clarification to value and how God looks at his people. His people are so important to him that he sent his only son to die on the cross for our sins and rose within three days for us to have life everlasting (John 3:16). kingdom value is how God sees us and not what the world thinks. Women of God, it is time to stand up and know your kingdom value. We all know of many stories (parables) in the Bible that talk about value. A very familiar story is the Jacob, Leah and Rachel.

The story of Leah is a powerful testimony. Many people don't know that even behind her gentleness was a woman that was on fire for God and knew that there was hope and desire. Although around her, people didn't see her value, even her father didn't see kingdom value. God ultimately saw it. He granted her six children with kingdom value. Leah went to God for each of her children with a prayer of value from the eyes of her husband. Although Jacob loved Rachel and she had two children, the kingdom value came from Leah through her son Judah. I am pretty sure she didn't know her son Judah would be a descendent in the line of Jesus Christ. Jacob didn't see Leah in all that she could offer nor did her sister Rachel, but God took her sorrow and made it into purpose (Genesis 29-31).

Women of God, the first way to understand kingdom value is seeing the potential. Leah was a woman who didn't understand her full purpose but understood that there had to be something special with a man who could speak to God. You may be in a place right now where you can't understand why. The next thing is to accept that there is a kingdom value in you. Finally, walk in your kingdom purpose, knowing there is value.

I am telling you it might seem like, at this moment, people have overlooked you. There may be moments when you feel like you have no value, but I'm declaring and speaking to you that God sees kingdom value in whoever you are. Your potential was given when Jesus died on the cross and rose again. The scripture says, "But you are a chosen race, a royal priesthood, a holy nation, a people for his own possession, that you may proclaim the excellencies of him who called you out of darkness into his marvelous light. Once you were not his people, but now you are God's people; once you had not received mercy, but now you have received mercy" (1 Peter 2:9-10).

Every person, at one time in their life, has experienced a Leah moment or will experience one. Leah did not know she was going to be the one that had the promise for the descendant's lineage of Jesus Christ. Although Jacob wanted Rachel, God said the promise was for the one that was unwanted.

My Leah moment has taken place countless times. One that I can remember is my high school years. My story is probably like many. I was picked on at school. I was told that nobody wanted me and that I was ugly.

"FOR I KNOW THE PLANS *THAT* I HAVE FOR YOU", DECLARES THE LORD "PLANS TO PROSPER YOU AND NOT TO HARM YOU, PLAN TO GIVE YOU HOPE " JEREMIAH 29:11

Girls would wait in the hall by the bus ramp just to make fun of me or could it have been the lack of the understanding their own value. I spent 4 years trying to bring an understanding to why my life was like this. Getting on the bus, I would prepare myself for a school day of cruel words, looks and comments. By my junior year, I believed every one of those words that were said to me. I didn't see any value in me.

Keep in mind, I was in the church, I had a supportive family and I was very active in church as well. I battled with value years after graduating high school. What was supposed to be a high school problem became a lifestyle for me. I walked around seeking my value through helping others fulfill their kingdom value. I was okay accepting whatever people labeled me to be and needed me to be. Then, a situation happened that knocked the wind out of me one day. Everything was out of control. I looked at one of my daughters after she mention that she believes in me. I realized then that I had to questioned where I was and how I felt about myself. I knew I had to regroup and bring some clarity to who I was in Christ Jesus. I realized I needed to know my value, not just for my children, my husband but for kingdom building. I had to accept that there was a kingdom value for me, God's value. Accepting kingdom value has brought

166

me to a whole new level of confidence, determination and most of all loving myself.

So, we speak life to you woman of God that you must put on what God has stamped you as. Know there's a kingdom value that you have, and it's time to walk in it in your life. It has been difficult and yes there has been brokenness. Yes, there has been things that you can't understand why it had to happen. Yes, the world will see you a certain way, but God sees you with kingdom value.

SUPPLICATION

Lord, we thank you for the love you have shown us. We thank you for dying on the cross for our sins. I will admit, Lord, that I have had my struggles with my value, my value in you. I know you have created me from the palm of your hands, and you have given me purpose. God, you said we are fearfully and wonderfully made, and I thank you for seeing the value in me when no one else does. I know you see your people with kingdom value. You see purpose, and I thank you for the opportunity to serve you. Thank you for your word that encourages us about our value and teaches us how to obtain it in you. We forever give you the glory and the honor. In Jesus' Name, Amen.

AFFIRMATION

I have potential.

I have value.

God has created me from the palm of his hands.

God sees kingdom value.

We are his children; we have purpose.

You are important.

We need you in kingdom building.

You are fearfully and wonderfully made.

APPLICATION

What's your value?

Write down a list of things that make you valuable. It cannot be an external attribute.

_____   _____

_____   _____

_____   _____

_____   _____

How can you use your kingdom value to make a great impact?

_____

_____

ABOUT THE AUTHOR

My name is Carissa B. I am a mother of 4 children and a wife of 18 years to Thomas B. I hold two degrees in Sociology and Criminal Justice. I am currently studying for a Masters in Praise/Worship. I have been in ministry for over 20 years, and I am working in the office of an evangelist. We have an active family ministry called TCB Ministries. We do a lot of outreach programs. I am a Branding/Management Resource Coach for Kingdom Relations Branding Music Group.

Currently, I am a radio programmer for 8 stations and an TV / radio network owner of Throne Connections Bridging Network. I own 5 award nominated radio stations. One of our radio stations is a women's radio station called "Behind the Brokenness." This is also the title for the women's conference we have annually as well.

Something I am passionate about is worshipping. I am a part of a multi-award winning group called, Not Easily Broken-NEBS.

Currently, I am writing a book called "Chronicles of a True Worshiper." I am forever grateful for every moment I get to service our Lord, and I'm so humble to be on this amazing journey with kingdom builders.

CONTACT INFORMATION

Email Address: Carissab2018@gmail.com

Website: www.tcbministries2019.com .

SOCIAL MEDIA

Facebook Page: @christ.like.33

Instagram: @carissabandnoteasilybroken

SURVIVAL OF A CHOSEN ONE
Jacqueline Lulu Brown

"Ye have not chosen me, but I have chosen you, and ordained you, that ye should go and bring forth fruit, and that your fruit should remain: that whatsoever ye shall ask of the Father in my name, he may give it you."

John 15:16

After Jesus stated how much he loved his disciples and that they had not chosen him, rather, he chose them (John 15:13-16), he faithfully acquainted them with the world's hatred of them, and what they must expect. His words did not imply any doubt about it, "If the world hates you." This was spoken as if they had some experience of it already and might look for more, when their master was gone from them. In order to engage their patience under it, he said, "Ye know that it hated me before it hated you." There is a survival kit required for those who are chosen.

I'm familiar with someone hating or disliking me. Moreover, I've experienced someone's distain based on my race. I was operating in my genius, showing up in excellence with compassion, integrity, and divine love. I made the decision early on in my Technology career that I would not compromise myself for gain. I was never going to become a corporate clone and certainly would never become part of the "good old boys." I stood on my God given gifts and dared to be different. I taught others to do the same, and it was by these basic principles that I became an excellent leader. I knew that I was chosen.

"I KNOW WHERE I'M GOING AND I KNOW THE TRUTH, AND I DON'T HAVE TO BE WHAT YOU WANT ME TO BE, I AM FREE TO BE WHAT I WANT"

MUHAMMAD ALI

My parents gave me two names, Jacqueline and Lulu, but; I'm fondly known as "Lulu." I was named Lulu after the endearing and mischievous cartoon character, Little Lulu. The character Lulu and myself had a lot in common; we were resourceful, resilient little girls who were very smart. The Lulu in me was viewed as "a piece of work." However, I rarely

171

initiate a battle unless provoked, but I do have an appetite to fight for justice and equality. This started at a young age, thanks to my oldest Sister, Denise. I was eccentric, referred to as a "busy body," imaginative and a talker. Mischief and trouble were never my goal but often the case. Over the years, I've learned to love and cherish my unique qualities and "crazy" imagination because therein is my genius. God gives us marvelous talents and gifts. It took years for me to appreciate my uniqueness and the power that resides within.

I always knew, in the deepest part of my heart, I was destined for greatness, however; I never spoke the words out aloud, and I certainly didn't envision that I'd carry a message to the masses of women that is often unpopular, yet necessary for growth and the ability for one to reach their highest elevation. More importantly, I didn't know that such a calling and being "chosen" would come with a major transformation and healing taking place in my life. My divine calling meant a willingness to hear the truth and go through my own process

"KNOW THAT YOU ARE CHOSEN AND STAND IN THE POWER AND AUTHORITY THAT COMES WITH BEING CHOSEN."

JLB
#THELULUEXPERIENCE

of awakening, self-discovery, reclaiming my self-worth, self-forgiveness, identifying my genius, operating in my authentic self, and allowing God to order my footsteps.

By the time, I was in my adolescent years, I was consistently living in what I later learned to be "fight-or-flight," a physiological reaction and response to stress. There were many traumatic experiences taking place in my family that kept me in the familiar fight-or-flight response for years to come as I normalized dysfunction. Domestic abuse between my parents resulted in my Mother's fall from a second story window. She survived but required a major brain operation and suffered other critical injuries. I witnessed family members suffering from drug addiction, alcoholism, and mental illness up close and personal. There was the absence of one or both parents during key adolescent periods, which brought feelings of abandonment. My dad was the more consistent figure in my life, however. In contrast to the negative exposures and traumatic experiences, I was being raised by my wonderful great-aunt and her husband. I was given to them at about 3 months old. This was my fraternal grandmother's sister. My father's side of the family were the "Cosby Show," only it was the

"NEVER UNDERESTIMATE THE DAMAGE OF WHAT A CHILD EXPERIENCES".

JLB

#THELULUEXPERIENCE

172

turbulent 60's. Everyone in my Dad's generation were educated, worked good jobs, and lived in nice homes. My grandmother's generation were classy, smart, and worked hard to provide the best they could for their family.

My father's mother and my aunts took us to church consistently. I knew there was a God, understood how to pray, was baptized when I was 8 years old and was on the Jr. usher board at church. However, I would not experience God in the form of a personal relationship with enlightenment until my late teenage years; my first husband was a Pentecostal pastor's son.

I met my first husband as a teenager in high school. His mother was immediately drawn to me. He was an only child, and his mother, a great Woman of faith and wisdom, always wanted a daughter. I became her daughter, and our relationship was that of Naomi and Ruth until she departed this life. My first husband's mother and father drew my mother to Christ with divine love. My mother became a great woman of God in the ministry. The insanity of my parents relationship dissolved. My Mother and Father became friends with a peace between them that surpassed everyone's understanding. My mother's prayers, faith, and deep relationship with God had her give the proclamation that God was going to save her daughters. This was manifested not many years after she spoke it. We became evangelist, missionaries, and elders. My mother is now 91 years old, and she remains active in ministry.

> "THEREFORE, WE SHOULD TAKE THE MOST EARNEST HEED TO THE THINGS WHICH WE HAVE HEARD LEST AT ANY TIME WE SHOULD LET THEM SLIP."
>
> HEBREWS 2:1

The blessings of God didn't come without pain and heart ache. When you are chosen by God, the enemy comes to kill, steal, and destroy. I went through turbulent times with my first husband. He was addicted to drugs and alcohol, and I suffered greatly while married to him. I had 3 small children, and there seemed to be no light at the end of my tunnel. I was immature in my relationship with God. The enemy set a trap, and I fell into it. My first husband and I parted. I was broken, bruised, and ripe for the enemy. I became involved in an abusive relationship and almost lost my life twice; yet again, there was that fight-or-flight on a consistent basis. This time it was fight-or-die.

There came a night that I decided to "fight and live." I'd had enough and either I would perish repenting, or God would bring me out of the bondage I'd become so entangled in. God told the enemy "she shall live and not die."

As the years went by, I grew in ministry. I enjoyed being used by God, and I loved doing anything that involved woman empowerment. The enemy was persistent on my trail, and I often made mistakes, but this time I persevered. I studied and received wisdom, knowledge and a better understanding of the Proverbs 31 Woman.

The years went on and the trials and tests grew stronger, but I continued to take the lessons learned and move forward in my purpose. In 2010, there was a strong shift beginning to happen in me. There was a heightened awareness in my spirit, driving me to go higher, deeper, and seek God's divine purpose for my life on a whole new level. By 2011, I received a deeper understanding of the things God downloaded in my spirit.

I was a high-flying corporate leader with tremendous success in my career of Information Technology and Engineering. Yet, I always knew corporate success was not my life's "true" calling, and there was more divine purpose to be discovered. At this time, God's purpose was burning inside of me like "fire shut up in my bones." In 2015, I began reaching out for guidance and help across all areas of my life: spiritually, intellectually, and mentally. My outcomes were self-discovery, reclaiming my self-worth, self-forgiveness, identifying my brilliance and genius, and bringing into alignment my spirit and authentic self. This was the inner work required before I could move on further. Too often, we are attempting to impart into others something we don't have ourselves. God's revelation showed me the need to transform the lives of professional women and help them come from living "behind the mask," a mask that I myself knew all to well and had broken through. I saw and accepted the assignment to revolutionize our Black churches by designing programs that addressed the unique needs of women from a God centered perspective of freedom and not the current chains that enslave us under the disguise of godliness.

> "POWER AND GREATNESS WAS IN ME WHEN I WAS IN MY MOTHER'S WOMB". "THE ENEMY IS UNABLE TO STOP GOD'S DIVINE PURPOSE AND DESTINY FOR MY LIFE.
>
> JLB
>
> #THELULUEXPERIENCE

Many people are not walking in their God given superpowers. Who they are authentically is not in divine alignment with their spirit. As people of God, we speak clichés about "the sky is the limit" when God has given us power, authority, and dominion over all things. There is no sky and there are no limits except the ones' that we create for ourselves. We need a radical approach to addressing the needs of women seeking their purpose. Many are called, but few are chosen. We must lead and minister with new insights about our feminine power, our divine gifts, and how to make radical positive change in the lives of others. I am a "CHOSEN SURVIVOR," and I know that every woman deserves a bright shining life that sings to their soul.

SUPPLICATION

God, I thank you in the name of Jesus for giving me the courage to answer your calling and accept your divine purpose for my life. I submit myself and acknowledge you in all my ways, asking that my path is divinely directed. As I go into prayer, I pray that, God, you will manifest your presence in my life. I humble myself before you. Thank you, God, because the weapons of my warfare are not carnal but are mighty to the pulling down of satanic strongholds. I pray that you will release legions of warrior angels to assist me in this battle. Let your angelic host bind and restrain every demonic resistance. Let them destroy every satanic opposition. God, I pray that you will dispatch special angels of battle to evacuate stubborn spirits and their agents to the land of the wicked for mass destruction by divine power. I put on your whole armor that I may withstand the wales of the enemy. In the name of Jesus, I've chose to take a stand against doubt, fear, and be strong and courageous as you've chosen me. I declare and decree that today, the angels of favor are released to favor me, and the angels of prosperity are dispatched to bring prosperity and abundance to me in the name of Jesus. I praise you, God, and offer up this prayer. Amen.

AFFIRMATION

I am victorious over every demonic hindrance. Sickness, disease, dis-ease, lack or want are not my portion.

I shall revolt against anything that tries to interrupt my destiny.

No weapon formed against me shall prosper.

I am prosperous.

I am whole.

I am enough.

I am brilliance.

I am a genius.

APPLICATION

Survive Being Chosen

We did not choose God. God chose us. Many are called, but few are chosen, and it comes with a price.

Write a Chosen Proclamation. In this statement, write down what you've had to survive to keep moving forward in God's purpose for your life and include the plan of action on how you will continue to survive the attacks of the enemy. In addition, list the victory promises (scriptures) of God.

Chosen by God Proclamation

I will survive and overcome (list the challenge)

_____
_____
_____
_____

To overcome my challenges, I will (Solution)

_____
_____
_____

Victory Scripture: Write scriptures from the word of God that you can stand on.

_____
_____

Who can you use as a resource to hold you accountable and hold you up?

_____

ABOUT THE AUTHOR

Jacqueline Lulu Brown, fondly known as "LuLu" is a dynamic woman who spent over 38 years in the Information Technology and Software Quality Engineering arena. During that time she held technical, management and executive leadership roles which allowed her to travel throughout the world in numerous countries that include the U.K., Australia, Israel, France, India, Span.

One of the things that "Lulu" discovered during her career and travels was that women in their career or business were feeling the heavy burden of silently carrying their "unsaid." These unsaid challenges are often not openly discussed because of secret shame, and ultimately, the fear of revealing one's true self. Through self-discovery, reclaiming her own self-worth, and lots of self-forgiveness work, she began showing up as her true authentic self, "Lulu".

Now, as a Transformational Speaker, Coach, Mentor, and Licensed Minister, she's spoken, coached, and mentored Women and Young Girls across the world, including India, the United Kingdom, Australia, Israel, Spain, Antigua, Mexico, and Aruba. Lulu's purpose and focus with her business, Revolution Ascension LLC, is to provide a safe space for open, honest and raw conversation. She and her team bring a comfortable, yet radical way of helping women see their greatness and brilliance in the middle of their challenges. Lulu values innovation, diversity, service, individuality, and equality.

Naturally philanthropic, "Lulu" also serves on multiple Boards; the "Precious Kids Foundation", as their Chief Program & Innovation Officer (CPIO) and is the Executive Director and COO for "The Way Out Ministries INC" a 501c3 corporation. She is married to Kevin Alan Brown with a blended family of six adult children, fourteen grandchildren and three great-grandchildren.

CONTACT INFORMATION

Email Address: jacquelinelulu@revolutionascension.com
Website: www.revolutionascension.com

SOCIAL MEDIA

Twitter: @RevolutionAsce1
Facebook Page: @revolutionascension
Instagram: @revolutionascension

THE BIGGER PICTURE
Karyn Munyai

---

*Consider it wholly joyful, my brethren, when you
are enveloped in or encounter trials of sort or fall
into various temptations*
JAMES 1: 2

I n life, we go through so many things; at the end, they make us to somehow believe there is no God, and there are specific people that God hears. This is not true. God hears and sees everything. He is always attentive to each and everyone's prayers. Our job is to wait on Him; at the right time, He will come through for us. King Jehoshophat was faced with so many battles in his life. He was worried about the army that was coming against him. When we read the Bible, we see that he first feared because each time we are faced with so many difficulties, the devil brings about fear, and he uses this thing called fear to make us see or feel that we can never become victorious, or we can never overcome the battles we face in this life. However, this king was wise enough to say, "I know I have all the powers to get all the kind of help I need, but I know the most powerful one I can go to and I know the owner will never let me down. He then went to GOD, His creator, the one who is the King of kings and the author and finisher of his faith. He said, "I know you can help me, and I trust no other god but you. After God answered Him, he went to his people and told them they needed to believe in the Lord, his God.

TO GRANT[CONSOLATION AND JOY] TO THOSE WHO MOURN IN ZIO – TO GIVE THEM AN ORNAMENT [A GARLAND OR DIADEM]OF BEAUTY INSTEAD OF ASHES , THE OIL OF JOY INSTEAD OF MOURNING ,THE GARMENT [EXPRESSIVE] OF PRAISE IN STEAD OF A HEAVY,BURDENED ,AND FAIING SPIRIT

ISAIAH 61:3

Sometimes we go through situations we can't get out of. It seems to come from all sides. What if God does not want you to come out of it? What if God is putting you in that situation for you to see his goodness at the end of it all ? What if He is, in fact, preparing you for greater places. If he takes you out of that situation, you might give birth to your miracle beforehand.

The Bible says that God wants to grant us consolation and joy, but we tend to not want the things that God is willing to give us because we think it is too difficult to handle or that we can never be able to overcome the temptations that comes with keeping it. However, we cannot understand God's love. Unconditional, and all he wants for us is to have peace and joy. He hates to see us in pain. He hates to see us having ashes of depression or unforgiveness. Letting go of things means having to give God everything that we are going through, those things we feel are stopping us from stepping into the fullness of God. You need to let it all go to God, and you will see how light you become and how happy things will be in your life, just let it all go and give it to God, just let Him be in control of everything. You don't need the heaviness or to feel down. He wants you to experience peace that surpasses all human understanding, only if you can just let Him in and see the kind of difference it will make.

THEREFORE GIRD UP THE
LIONS OF YOUR MIND BE
SOBER AND REST YOUR HOPE
FULLY UPON TH GRACE THAT IS
TO BE BROUGHT TO YOU AT
THE REVELATION OF JESUS
CHRIST

1PETER 1:13

PETERS audience was made up of hurting people . they were suffering persecutions from believers in the form of rejection, torture, imprisonment, and the threat of physical death. The price they paid for their beliefs, including everything from broken relationships and loss of employment, we go through seasons in our lives where we end up not knowing what God is busy doing during the seasons we are in. If you don't know the kind of seasons you are in, you will not know the kind of cloths or the kind of protections you need to have for you to be safe from the coldness that we are facing. There are dry seasons; these are the most dangerous seasons we face and the season where the enemy tries and tests us a lot.

During this season, we tend to want a quick fix so the pains we are facing may end fast. I remember when I was going through depression; I was so dry in my spirit that I wanted the pain to end. I was going around looking for a quick fix that would make things easy for me. When we are going through pain, we want to give up so fast that we forget if God is not done with us, we can never come out of the fire. For us to come out on the other side victorious, we need to go to the one who knows us, the one who told us he will never leave us nor forsake us. We need to invite God in our seasons. It is vital.

SUPPLICATION

Dear Lord, thank you for creating in me a clean heart, a heart that is going to be able to trust in you no matter the situations. I promise I will be totally depended on your word, for I believe it is life to my soul, and through your word, I will be able to prosper in everything I do. In Jesus' Name, Amen.

AFFIRMATION

I will trust God at all times.

I will do my best to love my enemies.

I will meditate on God's word every day.

I will love my self unconditionally no matter what people say about me.

APPLICATION

In life, we need to understand there are storms that will come. If we have a written agreement with God, it helps us to remember to trust Him through it all. You will notice that life will be easy because you are putting the source of your life in front of all that you do.

You can say this to yourself each morning I _____ promise to be faithful in everything I do in my life. I promise to trust God in everything, especially in the following areas namely_____,_____,_____. I will not let things like anger and………..and ………..to get to me. In Jesus' Name. Amen.

ABOUT THE AUTHOR

Karyn kone Munyai is the lat born daughter of Pastor Rd and Ns Munyai born and raised in South Africa. Pastor Karyn is a called evangelist, mentor, youth leader, motivational speaker and worshipper. She studied Travel and tour Operations and then went into teaching, which is her current profession. She has also faced many situations like depression, rejection, rape and suicide attempts that mad her decide to open her own foundation called Motivationalconnor Foundation, which helps young men and women in her community, who have or are going through similar situations. She believes if you invite God into every situation you are faced with, you come out on the other side victorious. Through these pages of her life, she hopes to motivate others that nothing is impossible with God if you let God in your environment.

CONTACT INFORMATION

Email Address: mandymunyai6@gmail.com

Website: wwww.motivationalconnor.com

SOCIAL MEDIA

Twitter: @motivationalconnor

Facebook Page: @motivationalconnor

BOSS LADY, BOSS MOVES
Alfreda T. Boney

She considers a field before she buys *or* accepts it
[expanding her business prudently];
With her profits, she plants fruitful vines in her
vineyard.
Proverbs 31: 16

T he Proverbs 31 woman, to many, exudes so many characteristics that to some would appear unmatchable to achieve. This was a woman that appears to have the best of both worlds. She has an amazing family and support system. Her husband is known by many. Therefore, they have an amazing reputation within the city. This keeps the family dynamic always in the spotlight. She has the wisdom and knowledge needed to take care of home and business and do so with much grace and integrity.

To go back to the beginning of the chapter, we must take in context the whole meaning of the reading. If you are anything like me, I was always told to aspire to be a "Godly woman" like our sister was described. But to read all that she exemplified, I gave up pretty quick! I mean, really? Who is that perfect?

From the first verse of this proverb, King Lemuel was being given wisdom from his mother on how to conduct himself as a king and rule over his constituents. She shared with him sound advice on the dos and don'ts of what was expected for a position such as his. Isn't it just like us as mothers to sit our children down and instill the wisdom of age and experience we hope will take them farther in life with less difficulty than how we traveled?

When we arrive to verse 10, it is his mother that is sharing how wise and amazing it will be to FIND a woman and companion that will be an asset to King Lemuel in his purpose as Leader. When I studied others' narratives of this same subject, I completely missed this perspective. You, too? LOL, we see only what we choose to see and sometimes what others would like for us to. So let's really look at this passage for all it was truly designed to give us as women to strive for.

Let me be transparent for a minute. I truly strive in my heart to represent myself in personal and business relationships as authentic and compassionate as I can be. I was not "raised" in the church as most have the testimony. I mean, my mother and father attended and made us go to Sunday school and third Sunday services and any and all revivals and homecomings and vacation bible schools that were scheduled.

I really connected with the Spirit of God when I was like 21-22, having just married and now a mother of 2 and stepmother of 1. I was expected to have a knowledge of how to run a home, take care of a husband and his needs/desires, take care of our children and their demands and somehow take care of myself with whatever was left. I had no manual or blueprint. I had a so so relationship with my mother. I mean, she loved me and my brother, but I found out in my late teens, early 20s that she only married our father in order to leave her home with its trials and scenes of abuse and turmoil.

FAILURE IS THE FERTILIZER THAT BLOOMS SUCCESS!

I always gravitated to older women during this season of life, to learn and engage and connect in order to grow into what I didn't originally have a model for. I learned the passion for business by watching professional women and how they carried themselves and gained respect and admiration from those in their circle. As a mother and still inexperienced in a lot, all I could do was dream of being greater than I was. It doesn't cost that much to dream, right? But oh the cost to walk in faith and believe for a change!

I have worked in a chicken plant, a carpet mill, summers as a teen in tobacco fields….I know what it is to work to make it do what it do, as the young people say. But to even begin to imagine that I would be in position today as an entrepreneur and mentor, coach and trainer, motivational speaker and now co-author? Back then, I would have truly laughed.

I see the attributes given to the Proverbs 31 Woman as a road map or blueprint for us to strive towards. King Lemuel's mother obviously was a wise woman of her years, so in order to describe the different facets of character that she desired her son to look for in his mate and future, she probably emulated them as well. We as women don't have to consider ourselves as less than just because we haven't arrived to this level of success or appearance thereof. Our goal should be to make everyday better by making small changes that will enhance our overall self, household and community.

When I looked at the example of the woman described, I paid attention to her abilities as a business woman and the fact that she never followed others opinions. She assessed the situation to make sure it was a benefit to herself as well as family. She took care of the needs of those who depended on her first. But she gave of her time and resources in order to make sure no one went without.

I started my business in 2008 as a need in my community to help those who desired to be self-sufficient and take care of themselves and family by obtaining gainful employment. I saw a need of educating others on how to present themselves on paper in the form of a resume as well as in person through a professional image and attire and communication during interviews. I really love assisting youth who are always told to just "get a job" but have no idea where to start, or with someone in transition out of prison or just in a different season of life and show them that they can start over.

I didn't make perfect decisions during this journey of self-awareness, at all. I had to make decisions that affected me and my children such as divorce, unemployment, sickness, parental deaths (both), and the list goes on. What I do know is that only by the grace and favor of God do I stand in my season of life now, still learning and growing and sharing that wisdom with others on how to stay the course and follow their passions.

Instead of looking at what you may not be yet according to the characteristics of the Proverbs 31 Woman, let's start with what you are and can be to gain confidence and success in your next phase:

1. She was confident, capable and self-assured. She was able to create and grow with what she had. You are so much more than what you appear to be. Trust God that you have everything you need to succeed and win in this season.

2. She believed in self-care FIRST! Verse 17 in the Amplified states, "She equips herself with strength [spiritual, mental, and physical fitness for her God-given task] And makes her arms strong." You are nothing to anyone else if you are nothing to yourself! I have been guilty recently of always being "ON" for everyone in Business and relationships, but "OFF" for myself. It's not healthy or beneficial. Take the time to take care of you. Everything else will fall into place.

3. She knows from where her help truly comes from. In everything listed that she is able to accomplish, it only came from her trust and dedication to God. To be honest, without her, nothing would be right in their world. You may not be a mother, Business

woman, or have a career yet, but you are so needed in this world for your unique gifts that God designed especially with you in mind for such a time as this. Don't sit on them waiting for that "special moment". Get up NOW and work with what you got. I didn't have a clue on how to run a business but through focus and follow through, meeting and learning different things from others doing what I desired, I took what I needed and made it my own. There's no need to compete with anyone since none of us actually perform in the exact same way. Be Uniquely YOU and watch God manifest the results!

The Proverbs 31 Woman was an amazing example of who we as women should always strive to be, in order to never become idle in our thinking, being and doing. Every woman has desires and dreams, hopes and passions that will help mold and create herself and those around her into their best position. As long as we keep God first in consideration of our decisions, (Psalms 16:8), there is nothing that we cannot achieve..

"IF YOU DON'T 'STAND OUT' THEN YOU WILL NEVER BE "OUTSTANDING!'

SUPPLICATION

Father **GOD**, we thank you for all that you give us to walk in this life. As women, we find ourselves more competing with each other than uplifting each other and assisting our sisters and others in becoming our best selves. You give us wisdom to ask for knowledge and strength and gave us faith to walk in favor and grace towards our destiny. Help us to know that all things work together for our good in every situation that you place before us; that you will perfect all things that concern us in family, business and community that we have a hand in. Show us our true purpose and passion in life that was created not just for us but for the world at large. We thank you for every gift and seed that was placed inside of us to use in your Kingdom. Like this model of virtuous servanthood, let us continue to strive to be the best in every area of life, not just a "Boss lady" in the board room but a "Boss lady" in life in general: owning our decisions and responsibilities to ourselves and others and making a difference every day. We love you, God, for your Mercy and aspire to walk in integrity and dignity from this day forward. In Jesus' Name. Amen

AFFIRMATION

I am a WOMAN with the ability to create something out of nothing and multiply what is given to me.

I am above only and not beneath; I compete with no one.

I am a leader who leads by example. I give in order to be a blessing which ultimately brings me blessings.

I walk by faith and not by sight.

I am who I am by the grace of God.

No weapon formed against me shall prosper: Life and Death are in the power of my tongue, and I choose to WIN.

I am a woman of valor.

I will live and not die to declare the works of the Lord.

APPLICATION

What are some characteristics that make you a Boss Lady in your world right now? Speak what you desire to see and be.

_____
_____
_____
_____
_____
_____
_____
_____

What are some steps you can take today to walk in your God given talents that will enhance your current household, workplace, business, community?

_____
_____
_____
_____
_____
_____
_____
_____

Create a Vision board for each month that will highlight some desires and ideas that you want to achieve before the end of the year. Remember, we can have what every we think and say. God will add the increase and make it even greater. Being a Boss is about owning your NOW! You are the only one that can control the outcome. No one else can dictate the outcome unless you give them the key and permission.

ABOUT THE AUTHOR

Alfreda T. Boney is the Founder and CEO of Perfectly Suited Career Consulting. With over 15 years of career development expertise in Recruitment/Staffing, Workforce Development, and Training, Alfreda has gained recognition in Career and Professional Development arenas to the young and old alike.

Her background includes knowledge of Labor Market Information, Unemployment policies and Workforce Development policies/procedures gained from employment with the Georgia Department of Labor; facilitator of Career Concepts training workshops with at-risk youth enrollees and graduates of the National Job Corps career training program; Management training in Leadership and Work Ethics and Etiquette; Certification as a Professional Résumé Writer from the Professional Association of Résumé Writers, recognized in the State of Georgia and nationally. She has conducted Business Etiquette and Employer Expectations workshops with various business classes at College of Coastal Georgia in Brunswick, GA and Re-Entry workshops with the City of Brunswick Weed and Seed Initiative and Operation New Hope/Ready4Work in Jacksonville, FL. She has been a partner and Co-Facilitator with Youth Development and career training with the National Youth on the M.O.V.E (Motivated to Obtain Valuable Employment) training program out of Atlanta, Ga. Currently, she has created and implemented the "Get Hired" and "#Work Ready" Career Training Platform, customized for Youth and Adult participants, as a Career Training and Professional Development event model to bridge the gap of communication between Jobseekers and Employers.

CONTACT INFORMATION

Email Address: aboney@perfectlysuitedcareers.com

Website: www.perfectlysuitedcareer.com

SOCIAL MEDIA

Facebook Page: @perfectlysuitedcareer consulting

Instagram: @Hrdiva_

INTIMACY IN MARRIAGE
Dr. Cheryl Kehl

Let your fountain be blessed, and rejoice in the wife of your youth, a lovely deer, a graceful doe. Let her breast fill you at all times with delight; be intoxicated always in her love. Proverbs 5:18-19

G rowing up in the church as a youth, I was made to believe that talking about sex and intimacy was not acceptable. God created sex to be enjoyable among a husband and wife. The world has perverted the subject, but it is still the will of God that a man enjoys his wife and a wife enjoy her husband. My mission is to have every Christian marriage get back to the fulfilling marriage that God intended us to have.

I have completed a course and have become a certified sex and intimacy coach with a focus on Christian marriages. I'm also certified to service clients in the way of relationship coaching with a biblical coaching program. The important thing to understand is that intimacy does not begin in the bedroom like many believe.

As children of God, He wants us to experience the best in every facet of our lives. The Bible tells men when they find a wife they find a good thing. If that is the case, why wouldn't God expect the man to enjoy his good thing in every possible way. Is it a man's responsibility to make his wife happy? I used to think that was one of the husband's responsibilities but found out later in life it is not. It is her responsibility to find the things that make her happy. So, a husband and wife should have open communication.

Communication is the first area I want to address in intimacy. Communication is extremely important in a marriage for it to be a happy and balanced marriage. When a marriage is in discord, it will be very hard for intimacy to be alive and well. Communication can be a hard area in the marriage to fix once there is a barrier. This is when it is important to have a third party to help get back on track. There are many exercises that will help in this area.

It took me many years to find out a third party could really help in this area of my marriage. A few years ago, when my husband and I were not agreeing on anything, we both just knew we were right. This caused a lot of stress and had us thinking a divorce was the answer. We did go for some marriage counseling. That helped a little, but we did not stay the course with her. I began seeking other options, and after a hard battle, I learned to use exercises to open the communication gates again. We learned we did not always have to agree but we at least needed to allow the other person to be heard.

We give no glory to the enemy, but he knows his job is to steal, kill and destroy. So he loves to destroy the family unit. After going through three divorces, I am on a war path to help save marriages. Often times, I allow too many things to get in the way and keep me busy. When I see his ugly head rise up, I stand my ground and start my war cry. My husband and I have pledged that we are in this thing until death do us part. We will continue to allow God to be the glue to hold us together. It all began with changing the way we communicate with each other.

Couples have to remember it is important to build in time to have fun together. In my coaching sessions, we discuss ideals on bonding and date nights. It is very important not to become bored with each other as this opens very dangerous doors. Sometimes as Christian couples, we forget to add this time in and spend too much time working and churching. Intimacy has to be intentional; it is too easy to overlook.

It is amazing how many couples remember their first date with details. But after many dates, they do not feel it is important enough to remember where they went. It is important to keep the fire burning in your marriage. Make each date or night as memorable as the first date. This is not impossible to do. Start by creating exciting date nights that keep the two of you close. Date nights should not be a routine thing that the couple is not looking forward to.

We always think that romance has to be expensive; that is not the case. Find things to do like a picnic somewhere. That would be unique and memorable. You may say, "I'm just not that creative." But you can go to a beach that is usually not on your list of things to do and have a picnic there. You can go to places that have great scenery and have things of interest to your spouse and take pictures together like you on a world tour. Think outside of the box and create memories together.

Think about some things you did as a teenager when spending time together with someone you liked. We did not have money back then most of the time, so we had to do things like go to the park and push each other on the swings while you laughed and talked about your dreams. Why do couples think they cannot do the small things that do not hurt the budget and still have fun now that they are married. It is because we have become so materialistic? We think the only way to have a really good time is to spend money traveling, eating out, going to plays and movies etc.

I remember the first time I spoke with my husband on the telephone. We must have talked for five hours straight. We invested the time to get to know each other before our first date. We have been married for thirteen years now, and we both have new interests, new dreams and goals. We have to still invest the time to talk about these things and be invested enough in each other to help the other meet those dreams. If you do not invest time in your spouse, there are walls that will be built that will cause you to drift apart. Do not allow this to happen.

HIS LEFT HAND IS UNDER MY HEAD, AND HIS RIGHT-HAND EMBRACES ME!

SONG OF SOLOMON 2:7

Spend some time together reading the Song of Solomon. He was so on point in how to keep the spark in his marriage. The Song of Solomon 2:7 reads, "His left hand is under my head and his right hand embraces me." He even shows us how we should cuddle in bed with our spouse. And people think that God's Word does not provide everything we need.

I spend a lot of time reading and listening to audio books about marriage. Kevin Lehman has a few books I love and recommend. One is Sex Begins in the Kitchen. He talks about how a couple should begin early in the day building up the suspense of a romantic evening.

One thing I have learned as a wife is that I need to communicate my needs to my husband. Men's brains are wired differently. Never take it for granted your spouse knows what you want. One thing that is important to know is there are so many things that have happened in our upbringing that plays on how we allow others into our hearts and how we display and receive love. The one thing is to be open, honest and patient. Our experiences are not other's experiences, and this may cause us to be misunderstood.

As stated before, take personal responsibility for your happiness, so you can become the wife God has ordained you to be. So many times, we are disappointed in our spouse because we have unrealistic expectations. Realize that we are not living in the fairytale fantasy we had as a teenager. We are two individuals, who mostly grew up in different lifestyles, coming together as one. The truth is you could have the best spouse in the world and still be miserable and unhappy because you are expecting them to fill a void they cannot. Sometimes, we may need to find our place in the world to be happy.

When I say find our place in the world, I mean find what we were created for. We cannot feel complete if we are not walking in our calling.

Another area I would like to address is spending time making you a better fulfilled person. If even, we need to create time to spend quality time as a couple, we also need personal time. In this personal time, we need to do self-improvement activities. This could include learning a hobby or taking educational courses. As women, we need to find time to pamper ourselves. Even pampering can be done on a budget. There are beauty schools that you can get a pedicure for $15. There are massage schools where you can get a massage for $30, and you can even enjoy a couple's massage together.

A very important thing is to have and show respect for each other. If you want to destroy a man's pride, disrespect him in front of people. This is the quickest way to destroy intimacy in any marriage. If you are anywhere near my age, you should remember a song from the group, the Beatles "All I Need Is Love." In my eyes, love is not enough. You have to love, honor, trust and respect your spouse. When any of these components are missing, there will be some strain in the marriage. This is what the Word of God says in Ephesians 5:33, "Each one of you must also love his wife as he loves himself, and the wife must respect her husband (NIV)."

One other thing I had to learn was to not be a nag to my husband. When we nag them, they sometimes see this as having too much criticism. This causes a man to shut down. Once he shuts down, it breaks the communication channels. If you are outspoken like myself, you will have to pray and ask God to help you learn when to be quiet. Our words have power, so when we say the wrong thing at the wrong time, they cause destruction.

When you start reading stories in the Bible how women prepared their bodies before going to their husband, you can learn from that. They spent many hours bathing and anointing their bodies with perfumes and precious oils. This gave me the idea of adding products to my business. We should still take the time to take care of our bodies and smell good when going to bed. We should also take the time to treat our skin to make sure it is soft and silky to the touch. There was so much given out in this chapter. I pray that God opens up our understanding on how to have intimacy in our marriages and enjoy each other. I am available for complimentary coaching sessions.

Each one of you must also love his wife as he loves himself, and the wife must respect her husband." (NIV)

SUPPLICATION

Dear God:

Thank you for the gift of marriage and for being the source of love. I pray that our union be known as a healthy loving union. Allow our actions towards each other to be an example of what a good Christian marriage should look like. Teach us to bear each other in love and grace in every situation we encounter. In areas that the enemy would try to dwell in our home, I ask that your will for us abide higher. Teach us to forgive each other and those around us. Help us to extend grace and walk in humility. Forgive us when we allow strife, bitterness and worry, to take root in our home. I ask that you replace quarrelling with compassion and joy. I pray we will be on the same page with one another as we walk out Your will for our marriage. I ask that you give us supernatural wisdom in everything that concerns us. Please give us discernment to know the right or wrong concerning our walk with you. I thank you that your plan for our marriage is always good. Allow us to continue to allow intimacy to be priority in our marriage. We love you and thank you for being number one in our marriage. Amen.

AFFIRMATION

1. MY MARRIAGE GROWS STRONGER EVERYDAY.

2. MY SPOUSE AND I WALK ON ONE ACCORD.

3. MY SPOUSE IS SUPPORTIVE OF ME AND ENCOURAGES ME TO FOLLOW MY DREAMS.

4. I AM FAITHFUL TO MY SPOUSE AND MY SPOUSE IS FAITHFUL TO ME.

5. MY MARRIAGE IS FREE FROM HURT, ANGER AND LACK.

6. MY MARRIAGE IS FULL OF ABUNDANCE, LOVE & COMPASSION.

7. COMMUNICATION IS KEY FOR MY SPOUSE & I.

8. MY MARRIAGE IS PRAYERFUL, POWERFUL AND PASSIONATE.

9. MY SPOUSE AND I ARE JUDGMENT FREE TOWARDS EACH OTHER.

10. MY SPOUSE & I LOVE EACH OTHER PASSIONATELY.

APPLICATION

Some   creative ways I will add date night to our calendars:

_____

_____

_____

_____

Read the Song of Solomon with my spouse.

_____

_____

_____

_____

Make an agreement to silence the electronics when we are sharing dinner together.

What day have we dedicated to prayer and reading together whether it is a book on marriage or the Bible?

_____

ABOUT THE AUTHOR

Cheryl Kehl is a wife, mother of 6 and grandmother to 10. Cheryl was born in Trenton, New Jersey and moved to North Jersey to East Orange at the age of twelve where she finished her schooling. After graduating and marrying and becoming a mother, she decided to join the United States Air Force Reserve. She loved the military life and decided to go active duty with the United States Navy. The Navy stationed her in Jacksonville, FL which is now where she calls home. Cheryl is a Licensed and ordained pastor with I Am A Ruby Global Ministries. She is also licensed as a chaplain with Chaplain Fellowship Ministries and serves as a volunteer chaplain at Duval Correctional Facilities. Cheryl is currently very active in ministry at her church serving as a Care Team Member, Middle School Ministry as a disciple group leader and connection team member.

Cheryl is a multiple business owner and loves serving people. She is a Certified Christian Life Coach with At The Table Coaching, Certified Intimacy Coach with The Dr. Rachel Institute and Relationship Coach with Transformation Academy. She is currently enrolled in 2 additional life coach certification programs to enhance her skills. Cheryl is also a Certified Travel Agent, Licensed Real Estate Agent and Life Insurance Agent. Cheryl is also a Certified Facilitator with Prepare and Enrich where she has learned how to help couples strengthen their relations pre and post marriage. Cheryl is the founder and relationship coach with E.M.P. (Empowering Couples With Purpose). The sole purpose of E.M.P. is to empower couples to have a thriving marriage where they can serve God and be an example of healthy marriages.

CONTACT INFORMATION

Email Address: cherylkehl@gmail.com

SOCIAL MEDIA

Facebook Page: @emp2020

DO NOT ABORT YOUR PURPOSE BEFORE IT IS BIRTHED

The Inner Woman Relay Team

Stay In Your Lane

Annette Bee

"Before I formed you in the womb I knew you, and before you were born I consecrated you: I appointed you a prophet to the nations"
Jeremiah 1:5

On Your Marks!!!

We were formed in our mother's womb, and from the moment we were formed God had a purpose for our lives. We were strategically placed in a family unit or in some cases, not. Born into a loving family, born into a family where you were wrapped in a piece of fabric and left on a cold doorstep whether in love or rejection or even born a princess. All we know for certain, our lanes were chosen for us and determined before conception.

Get Set!!! Prestigious

As a wife, mother, glammother or grandmother if you prefer, an entrepreneur, a psalmist/song writer and more importantly a Christian woman, knowing my purpose was crucial to my survival in my Christian walk, my family life and my entrepreneur world. Certain challenges in life can bring us to a low ebb. Since becoming a Christian the fire got hotter hypothetically speaking. Sometimes the challenges faced cut so, so, so deep, suicide; murder or a complete mental breakdown could easily of been my portion. BUT GOD!!! My purpose could have been aborted before it was even birthed; however, I knew my worth. Just like you, I was worth far more than rubies. The adversities we face can scramble the waves of connectivity we have that aligns us to God. Our past and current situation can distract us from our purpose. We may of experienced physical abuse, domestic abuse, sexual abuse, modern slavery, organizational abuse, psychological and emotional abuse, been neglected, rejected, struggled with drug addiction, alcohol addiction, experienced prolonged illnesses, a miscarriage, a marriage breakdown, a life of crime and so on, but I am here to tell you, while we have breath, let us hang on tight to our faith (as my dear friend would say) like a drowning man hangs on to a float, for whilst we have breath we have HOPE, and having HOPE will help us to COPE in any situation. These attacks are clearly from the enemy, his strategy to take us off course, out of our lane and out of our purpose. The enemy knew his purpose but allowed greed and jealousy to take him out of his lane down to hell.

Go!!!

Go and fulfill your purpose. What is your purpose? Evaluate yourself, then re-evaluate again. Seek God and you will find. This is especially for the married woman and mother. Ensure you strike a balance when executing your purpose. The Proverbs Woman, who is "a wife of noble character," (Proverbs 31:10) exudes a warm, loving, caring and nurturing quality. She has the ability to multitask, she's a wife, she looks after the children, she's a homemaker and the list goes on. I know this is something a lot of us women can relate to. Whatever our purpose is there are a few common denominators in how we execute our calling: being able to articulate, work diligently, work smarter as opposed to harder.

If you are an entrepreneur, being able to communicate to your target audience is a must to achieve the desired end result. 'She sees that her trading is profitable, and her lamp does not go out at night." If you are a prayer warrior you have to be able to communicate with God to petition and intercede on someone's behalf. The virtuous woman "speaks with wisdom, and faithful instruction is on her tongue" (Proverbs 31:26). You may have speech impediments, or may not be able to speak at all. That's ok. Speaking verbally is not the only form of communication, so don't allow anything or anyone to stop you from fulfilling your purpose. Ester's husband had full confidence in her and lacked nothing of value. She worked vigorously and she knew her worth. Just like Esther, knowing your purpose helps you to focus your aim, causing you not to be aiming aimlessly. Strategic planning to execute your purpose is a must, 'And the Lord answered me, and said, "Write the vision, and make it plain upon tables, that he may run that readeth it" (Habakkuk 2:2 (KJV). Surround yourself with like-minded Christians who can cover you in prayer, for at times we have to walk the journey alone. Incubating in God's arms is a must, for it is comforting, it realigns us and reassures us that He is Abba Father. I could have easily been one of those statistics if it were not for the grace and the love of God. Just like Esther, she was born a Jew, which was frowned upon in certain parts of the world. Jews were made to feel ostracized and like the underdog, an experience a lot of us face today in our world.

Let us change the landscape of our lives; get back into your lane where the grass is greener. You see, God is our life coach, our trainer, our guide, and he directs us how to get over hurdles in our lane. Note, He did not remove the hurdles; however, He helps us to get over them, just like the three Hebrew boys. He will send wise people to guide us, to train us, to have values, good ethics, but most importantly to know God.

How we train our mind, body and soul, has a direct impact on our day-to-day performance. If our daily intake is not edifying to our body as a whole we become disillusioned, sluggish, give up and go outside of our lane. Often times God places us in positions in front of people and in places we deem out of our lane, but unknown to us, that issue, that person and that bad or good experience was placed in **our** lane to help train and build us up for **our** destination which is to *be in alignment with God's purpose for us.*

We have a saying 'Don't allow your past to determine your future' just like Esther who saw opportunities to become a queen. God put Esther in her lane. She was a Jew, a nationality that was not accepted. She was a woman. She experienced bereavement at a young age losing not one but both of her parents; she was an orphan. She could have easily "gone off the rail" so to speak. Esther may have been the only Jew in the lineup of potential brides for the king, however, God strategically placed her to be chosen.

Let's look at Ester in the Bible a little more. As Esther, who was riddled with fear when positioned to ask the king not to kill the Jews, we too can attack our hurdles with God at the centre. Unforeseen hurdles we stumble across in our lane may bruise us, but you just have to keep fighting.

Esther was prompted by Mordaci to approach the king without an invitation. She rose to the challenge to save her people; she was bold when she approached the king to make a request knowing that she could be killed for not being invited by him. Her boldness saved the Jews from being slaughtered because of her request to the king to save the Jews. She also exposed her true Jewish Nationality knowing this could have been fatal. We should take up the mantel in our lives in spite of what curveball life has thrown at us.

Esther had a good role model, a good counsellor, someone who was wise and guided her accordingly. We too need quality people in our lives that give good counsel. Following our purpose may plant us in places that are controversial, however God would not take us into a situation without bringing us through it. Sometimes we have to be bold, sharpen our communication skills, believe in ourselves and be confident. She put her heartache and concerns before God, informed Mordaci to tell our people to fast for 3 days and 3 nights so the plot to kill the Jews was aborted.

YOU DID NOT CHOOSE ME, BUT I CHOSE YOU AND APPOINTED YOU THAT YOU SHOULD GO AND BEAR FRUIT AND THAT YOUR FRUIT SHOULD ABIDE, SO THAT WHATEVER YOU ASK THE FATHER IN MY NAME, HE MAY GIVE IT TO YOU.

Whatever our past, because of the grace of God we can be healed and aided to walk in our lane. Your hurricane season may be treacherous, and if it feels like it is never going away, reach into the eye of the hurricane where it is calm. There days when we just need to be still. Jesus will be there to protect you, for this too will pass.

The Inner Woman 1: At the painful start of your race, you were crouched down at the line, with a heavy baton; you may still be at that line right now. You are broken in several places, mentally, emotionally and physically. You are in a position waiting for someone to tell you to go, get up and run. That someone is Jesus. However, at the same time, the enemy is whispering in your ear to lie down and die. There is a fuzzy noise that is going around in your head, a distraction, a blockage, a feeling of heaviness inside. Let us pray without ceasing and refer to the word for strength, for this too shall pass. Jesus's voice will penetrate through and you will hear Him more clearly as you start to rise. 'But rise and stand to your feet, for I have appeared to you for this purpose, to appoint you as a servant and witness to the things in which you have seen me and to those in which I will appear to you,' (Acts 26:16).

The Inner Woman no 2: YOU receive the baton which is still painful, but hey, you are listening to and relying on your trainer, Jesus Christ. YOUR strength increases, you gather more speed, and your off and running. YOU are now becoming more upright, and this is the second part of your healing journey. YOU are the one with the insight into your life; with God's grace, you are the one that can change your life and go on to change the lives of others who find themselves in the same scenario. YOU can make a difference. Athletes have to deny themselves certain things from their diet, they have to plan their exercise routine, and they have to be disciplined and focus on what is ahead of them. "The heart of man plans his way, but the LORD establishes his steps" (Proverbs 16:9). Just as the scripture says, let us plan our way but allow the LORD to establish our steps.

The Inner Woman no 3: Now it is time to dig your heels in, grit your teeth and run with purpose. Your wounds are now scars, reminding you where you came from and where God has brought you too. Take time to reflect on your journey, for it has not been easy; enjoy God's presence and guidance. The family member who abused you, pray for them. The bullying that took place at your work place, just place them in the hands of the Lord. For no weapon formed against you shall prosper. Woman number 1 and 2 are way behind you, you are in a good place. Be proactive with your gifts and your purposes, for God chose you to receive these wonderful gifts and purpose. "You did not choose me, but I chose you and appointed you that you should go and bear fruit and that your fruit should abide, so that whatever you ask the Father in my name, he may give it to you." John 15:16. What an honour!!

The **Inner Woman no 4:** Last leg and last lap. Now that you've searched and found your purpose, the finishing line is in sight. Stay on course, keep God in the center of your lives and let us continue fulfilling our purpose. We are fully in charge with God at the center. Unfortunately obstacles will be our portion and this is because satan wants to take us out of our lane again. This is to be expected so do not be to alarmed, just see it for what it is.

He will use anyone and everyone to trip us up causing us to stumble and fall. He will use our mother, father, siblings, friends, work colleges, church brethren and the list goes on. Just remember to see it for what it is. At times I stumbled but God prevented me from falling and for this I am eternally grateful.

If however you do fall, reach up and allow God to reach down and pick you up. For you may be down but you are not OUT.

YOUR Lane Is Your Purpose, Stay In YOUR Lane, Stay In YOUR Purpose

Chapter 5

Finish Line!!!

1 Peter 1:6-7 New International Version (NIV) "⁶ In all this you greatly rejoice, though now for a little while you may have had to suffer grief in all kinds of trials. ⁷ These have come so that the proven genuineness of your faith—of greater worth than gold, which perishes even though refined by fire—may result in praise, glory and honor when Jesus Christ is revealed."

I was anxious about writing this chapter, but I allowed God to guide me and complete my purpose.

YOUR Lane Is Your Purpose, Stay In YOUR Lane, Stay In YOUR Purpose

SUPPLICATION

Father, I thank you in the name of Jesus for giving me the courage to revolt against my oppressor. I know that there is liberty in you, and I chose to serve you alone. Lord, I admit that I have no strength to deliver myself from under the hand of my enemies. But I know you do; therefore, I humble myself unto you in the name of Jesus. You said in your word that no weapon that is formed against me shall prosper and that every tongue that rises up against me shall be condemned. Because I believe in you, I know that the weapon of jealousy, psychological, mental and physical abuse, shall not prosper in my life. I bless you for delivering me from every form of oppression that has launched an attack against my purpose, visions, and dreams. I put on the whole armor of God that I may withstand the wales of the enemy. In the name of Jesus, I choose to take a stand against my oppressor and be strong and courageous. I declare and decree that my enemy is a defeated foe and that my oppressor does not have the strength to defeat me. I am more than a conquer in Christ Jesus. You are a faithful Father, and I love you. It is in the majestic name of Jesus that I praise you and offer up this prayer. Amen.

AFFIRMATION

I shall live in the Freedom of Christ Jesus.
I am victorious over my oppressor.
I shall not live under oppressive conditions.
I shall trust God and revolt against anything that tries to oppress me.
I AM graced to WIN.
I can do all things through Christ that strengthens me.
No weapon formed against me shall prosper .
I am successful.
I am whole.
I am accepted in Christ Jesus.
I am enough.

APPLICATION

WRITE THE VISION

Write your personal vision statement based upon Gods purpose for your life.

Determine what training you need to get in shape to run the race that God has marked out for you.

Run with your God ordained vision.

ABOUT THE AUTHOR

Annette Bee is a Multi-Award Winning Secular Artist, Multi Award Winning gospel Artist, entrepreneur, and the founder of Gospel Xplosion Ministries which hosts The GX Gospel Awards UK.

In 2001, Annette gave her heart to the Lord, however she did not start recording again until 2006. Annette Bee has received multiple gospel awards for her singing and for what she has accomplished in the community for championing peace. She was voted UK's Best Female Reggae Gospel Singer for 2014 at the Prosperity Music Awards and also nominated for a BEFTTA Award for Best Gospel act in 2014. Annette Bee picked up three gongs at the Gospel XPLOSION Music Media Awards UK in 2016, when she won the Best Female Reggae Gospel Artist Of The Year, Best TV Show [Annette Bee's Gospel Xplosion Segment on The Lifestyle Show on BEN TV Sky 182], and Best Female Artist of the Year. The organization International World Peace Group awarded Annette The Peace Award for fighting against gun & knife crime. Annette also won best Reggae fusion at the Akademia Awards in Los Angeles in 2016. Annette's passion, outside of her singing and media ministry, is taking care of people whom have suffered with mental health issues, as well as supporting people who have experienced domestic abuse.

Annette is an MBA graduate, and uses her passion and qualifications to help others.

CONTACT INFORMATION

Email Address: info@annette-bee.com

SOCIAL MEDIA

Twitter: @annettebee_

Facebook Page: @AnnetteBee

Instagram: @annettebee_

FROM BEHIND THE MASK TO THE VALUE OF AUTHENTICITY IN GOD

Jacqueline Lulu Brown

"For his eyes are upon the ways of man, and he seeth
all his goings."

Job 34:21

We all struggle with the temptation to wear masks, and it's a lifelong struggle. We face temptations regularly, often daily, to try to be someone we're not. Whether we are just trying to fit in, attempting to hide our hurts with the "I'm fine" mask, or doing whatever it takes to make others like us, the struggle is real. Since this temptation is common to all people, we are in good company!

I think you could even make a case that Jesus was tempted to wear masks; in the Bible it says that Jesus was tempted in every way that we are, but never sinned. So, even though Jesus experienced the temptation to be fake, He never was. He was Himself all of the time. By looking to Him, we can find help and inspiration as we strive to be true to ourselves.

"GOD SEE'S BEHIND THE MASK WE WEAR"

JLB

#THELULUEXPERIENCE

A few points to get us started:

- When Jesus was sad, He cried. He didn't wear the mask of being a tough guy who doesn't express emotions (John 11:35).
- Jesus celebrated special occasions; He knew how to have a good time. He went to a wedding reception, and there He turned water into wine (John 2:1-11).
- When Jesus was scared, He prayed. He knew He needed help and was willing to ask His Father in Heaven (Matthew 26:36-39).
- When Jesus needed others, He asked His friends for help. He knew He needed other people (Matthew 26:38).
- When Jesus saw people who needed a friend, He hung out with them. He wasn't afraid of what others might think (Luke 5:29-32).

The above are just a few examples. We can find a lot more examples of Jesus being mask-free in the Scriptures. As a matter of fact, his whole life is a beautiful expression of mask-free living!

I am aware of masks and wearing them well. My life of wearing masks began when I was five (5) years old on the day of my birthday party. I was being raised by my wonderful great-aunt and her husband. I was given to them at about 3 months old. Both spent a great deal of time and effort to make my birthday party special. The setting was elegant for a five (5) year old's party with lace tablecloths, fancy china, crystal candy dishes, and a professional photographer. Adults and children were dressed "too the nine" as they say. My dad, grandmother, and sister looked exceptional. There was one very important issue for me, however; my mother was missing. She said she would be there but on the day of my party as my aunt presented me *with* a beautiful dress from my mom, I was informed she would not be at my party. My heart was broken, and I suddenly didn't care if there was one. I was reminded of how much effort was put into this elaborate party for me and how grateful I should be. I swallowed my heartache, put on a happy face, and remained joyful until that night when I cried myself to sleep. I didn't realize, at the time, that this was the beginning of my "Unsaid" and learning to live behind a mask.

> "MIRROR MIRROR ON THE WALL WHO IS THE LITTLE PRINCESS IN PAIN FROM IT ALL".
>
> JLB
>
> #THELULUEXPERIENCE

My *paternal* grandmother and her siblings were a proud and proper family. The women were "rocks of Gibraltar" that consistently stood the storms of life, trials, and tribulations, never missing a beat. These women walked in a strength that only God could provide. Family issues, challenges or problems were never worn on their sleeve; rather, these women had a mask of pure strength and perfection. One could see a glimpse of our lives from the outside only. These women never displayed weakness and clearly ruled the throne of our family with excellence. My grandmother battled mental illness over the years, yet I saw more of her strength than the perceived weakness. As the years passed, I was gifted with God's wisdom to see that her broken heart (a result of my grandfather) was at the root of her challenges in life. Yet, my grandmother never displayed weaknesses that I was able to interpret as such, and her spirit stayed strong as she helped to raise one of my sisters and also helped take care of me, my sister and our cousins on a daily basis after school.

I learned at a very young age that there are some things one does not mention or talk about. We bury it deep within; we harness it and control it rather than it controlling us. As an example, my paternal great Aunt, Minerva, never complained. At the time she married my uncle, she was unable to have children due to a hysterectomy at a young age. She wanted children and was blessed to have my father show up with me on her doorstep at three (3) months old. She was already 50 years old and not in the best physical condition, yet she took me with open arms. She was also the "go-to" person in the family. Many sought her council (often secretly) when financial help or advice were needed. She was certainly the person everyone went to during a crisis. Little did I know, when this behavior is not channeled and utilized appropriately, it turns into "mammy syndrome" and "co-dependency."

As I approached adult life, all the other "unsaid" in my life began to manifest, and I continued to hide all of it behind a mask. I'd never witnessed any of the strong women in my family exhibit their true feelings or express what they were "really" going through at a given moment. I saw tough, strong, "put the better on the outside" type behaviors. I normalized this and became an expert at mirroring what I saw in others. If it worked for them, it had to work for me.

Throughout my life, I often questioned my sanity as I was intelligent enough to realize that I was suffering from a wave of unexpressed emotions that began to manifest during my childhood. As I was approaching 50 years old, I realized that the maze of emotions behind my mask must be uncovered, resolved, and killed at the root. I often felt frustration, sadness, isolated, weary, manipulated, shame, depressed, hostile, used, overwhelmed, stressed, a failure, and I had little or NO self-worth. I married for the second time at age 42 (which I brought a truck load of emotional pain and baggage into), and I'd already experienced mental and physical abusive relationships before I reached 26 years old.

I'd developed multiple personalities to fit any occasion. As an example, I was type A+++ at work and in my career. Moreover, I could easily bounce back into my natural self, which are "Water" and "Air" personality types.

As I took a harsh, honest look at myself, I realized that while I found great success in my career and business, I also felt the heavy burden of silently carrying my "unsaid." These unsaid challenges were never openly discussed at a level required because of secret shame and, ultimately, the fear of revealing my true self. After all, I was "Lulu" the crazy one! I was outrageous in my thinking and many thought I lived in a "fantasy land" because I thought differently, had a distain for the "status quo," and simply knew in my heart that my outrageous dreams were obtainable.

This incredible woman, Lulu, was everything to everyone, and yet I felt the strain of my own mental, physical, and emotional neglect. I was giving to everyone else until there was nothing left for myself. I was quick to forgive others, but I was my own harshest critic. This was the model set for me and all the women in my generation, however; I dare not speak such critical words about the Elders (those strong women) from my grandmother's generation.

Despite difficulties, and challenging times, my professional life thrived. I spent over 38 years in Information Technology. During this time, I held technical, management, and executive leadership roles.

I balanced my career and traveled the world while holding strong in my position as one of many strong women in my family. And, while I was deemed successful by societal standards, I knew in my heart that I had not reached my "limitless" abilities. The barrier between "success" and "limitless" was my "unsaid" and breaking free from behind the mask. I'd show up at my professional career, "dressed to the nine," on point, with "knock it out of the park" presentations and solutions, and often performing better than my peers, yet; I was broken on the inside with my personal life in shambles. I remember there were bags of unopened mail on my table and bills often went unpaid even though I had money in my account to pay them. This held equally true in my spiritual life. I could minister to women on a level that was life changing, yet again; I remained lacking in many areas of my own spiritual life.

> "Brilliance Is Hidden Behind Our Masks Because Of Our "Unsaid."
>
> JLB
>
> #theluluexperience

They say when you hit 50 something changes in the brain. This was very true for me. I remember knowing and feeling my true calling and genius burning like "fire shut up in my bones." But I also knew I was living a life of unresolved issues, pain, and un-truths. Prayer was always my greatest strength and to this day I believe it is part of my DNA from both my grandmothers, therefore; my conversations with God began to change. I began seeking God on a level that blew my own mind.

I set out on a path to grow beyond "worldly" or "society's" success. I sought professional help spiritually, mentally, and began to change my business and social circles. I embraced my crazy for therein is my genius. I removed negative "naysayers" from my ears. I became tone deaf to anything that was contrary to where I knew I was destined to go. Through self-discovery, reclaiming my self-worth, and a lot of self-forgiveness work, I began showing up as my true self. I confronted every demon behind my mask. The biggest demon behind my mask was self-denigration. I stopped allowing people to take my self-worth, which is something that many confuse with self-esteem. They are two different things and manifest themselves differently in our lives for better or worse. I removed the worse and stepped into the better.

Negative behaviors such as emotional eating, living in constant "fight-

or-flight" mode were destroyed at the root and removed from my life. Confession, truth, and recovery were my path forward. I set some major critical success factors:

✓ A consciousness, to connect with my soul's deepest purpose.
✓ Kill mammy.
✓ Love Myself as God Loves Me.
✓ Walk in my Brilliance.
✓ Know My Worth.
✓ Embrace My Crazy Because It's My Genius.

After taking myself through a rigorous process, there were five (5) key outcomes and things that people should know about me:

1. My vibrational frequency is high energy, dynamic, and uplifting.
   I'm a go-getter with a fire in my belly for prayer, transforming lives, and making a meaningful impact on others. And, I'm a great storyteller. I love being a great hostess and entertainer.

2. I love to travel and experience the world around me.
   My destinations included India, the United Kingdom, France, Australia, Dubai, Israel, Spain, and many of the British Islands. That said, my favorite place of all is Aruba. It's where my husband, Kevin, and I were married. It was his support in our home life that made traveling the globe for my career and worldwide leadership responsibilities possible.

3. I embrace my crazy, wild and (sometimes) foolish imagination.
   Growing up, I was constantly called crazy, busy-body, loud, outrageous, confrontational, noisy, disruptive. I was told that the things I believed possible were impossible. Over time, I allowed this message to diminish my outrageous dreams. But no longer. I've discovered what some deemed as 'crazy' was and is my genius.

4. I'm driven by love. Love for God, love for my family, love for great conversation with incredible people, and love for delicious food. Only the strength of love could have helped me overcome the obstacles I've faced in my life. It inspires me, encourages me, and motivates me to continue spreading my God inspired messages.

5. I believe that we as women are limitless. Here's the truth: there are no limits in our greatness. That thing holding us back, it is our "unsaid." It's the gate blocking our way and we simply need to look inside to find the key.

Every woman deserves a bright shining life that sings to their soul. My goal is to support and guide professional women through their journey of self-discovery and reclaiming their own self-worth, so that they are free from the obstacles that hold them back. This work energizes me, pulls me forward, and ignites my soul. This work is both my purpose and my legacy, and it's what I want to be remembered for most.

Let's check our alignment with our inner truth, our spirit, and come from "behind the mask." We sometimes lose touch with our "true self." Are you ready to reveal your "true you" and live boldly without limits?

Since Jesus never wore masks, He can help us to resist the temptation to wear masks. So, when you struggle with masks, as we all do, ask Jesus to help you. And, He will! Two of my favorite prayers are "Jesus, make me into the person that you created me to be" and "Lord, help me to be the best version of myself."

SUPPLICATION

God, I thank you in the name of Jesus for giving me the courage to seek out and find the world's most unusual therapist and spiritual counselors. In the name of Jesus, I've chosen to come from behind the mask and stand against doubt, fear, and be strong and courageous. I

> "YOUR PATH IS CREATED IN THE MOMENT OF ACTION"
>
> JLB
> #THELULUEXPERIENCE

embrace the process of repentance, forgiveness, and transformation. I accept deliverance from negative energies and toxic emotions. I praise you God and offer up this prayer. Amen.

AFFIRMATION

I use positive micro messages (micro advantages) to spark creativity, improve my performance in life, and exceed God's goals for my life.

I shall revolt against anything that tries to interrupt my destiny.

I am not bound by the limits of this world, rather; I am limitless and can do all things through Christ Jesus that strengthens me.

APPLICATION

Come from Behind Your Mask: Confession – Truth – Recovery:

Write a Proclamation. In this statement, write down what's behind your mask. In addition, list the victory promises (scriptures) of God that you can stand on.

Who can help hold you accountable and support you? Identify resources that will help you remain in deliverance.

ABOUT THE AUTHOR

Jacqueline Lulu Brown, fondly known as "LuLu" is a dynamic woman who spent over 38 years in the Information Technology and Software Quality Engineering arena. During that time she held technical, management and executive leadership roles which allowed her to travel throughout the world in numerous countries that include the U.K., Australia, Israel, France, India, Span.

One of the things that "Lulu" discovered during her career and travels was that women in their career or business were feeling the heavy burden of silently carrying their "unsaid." These unsaid challenges are often not openly discussed because of secret shame, and ultimately, the fear of revealing one's true self. Through self-discovery, reclaiming her own self-worth, and lots of self-forgiveness work, she began showing up as her true authentic self, "Lulu".

Now, as a Transformational Speaker, Coach, Mentor, and Licensed Minister, she's spoken, coached, and mentored Women and Young Girls across the world, including India, the United Kingdom, Australia, Israel, Spain, Antigua, Mexico, and Aruba. Lulu's purpose and focus with her business, Revolution Ascension LLC, is to provide a safe space for open, honest and raw conversation. She and her team bring a comfortable, yet radical way of helping women see their greatness and brilliance in the middle of their challenges. Lulu values innovation, diversity, service, individuality, and equality.

Naturally philanthropic, "Lulu" also serves on multiple Boards; the "Precious Kids Foundation," as their Chief Program & Innovation Officer (CPIO) and is the Executive Director and COO for "The Way-Out Ministries INC" a 501c3 corporation. She is married to Kevin Alan Brown with a blended family of six adult children, fourteen grandchildren and three great-grandchildren.

CONTACT INFORMATION

Email Address: jacquelinelulu@revolutionascension.com
Website: www.revolutionascension.com

SOCIAL MEDIA

Twitter: @RevolutionAsce1
Facebook Page: @revolutionascension
Instagram: @revolutionascension

MY PAIN GAVE ME MY TESTIMONY

Shameka Jones

"Before I formed you in the womb I knew you,
before you were born I set you apart; I appointed
you as a prophet to the nations."
Jeremiah 1:5

Life wasn't easy for me at all. I had to endure many painful events in my life dealing with rejection, abandonment, abused, and depression that left me feeling like I was nothing. I was never shown the proper love. However, God was there. He held my hand every step of the way even though at times I didn't feel like He was still there. He always protected me from my enemies. He always loved me when I felt like no one else did. In his word, it says I will never leave you nor forsake you, nor leave you begging for bread.

Much of my childhood is a blur because I cannot remember what took place. My therapist told me I have memory blockage due to my traumatic upbringing. I can believe the truth in what she is saying because my aunt would make mention of my childhood and how they were worried about me. As a little girl, I was mute. My mode of communication was making noises and pointing toward things to let others know what I wanted.

One day, they took me to church, and I received prayer. After prayer, my mouth began to open. Praises be unto God because He still causes the mute to speak. God was already working miracles in my life as a child, and I thank Him in advance. Thank you, Jesus.

I did not receive the proper love and care from my mom growing up. She was very mean and said hurtful thing to us. I understand she had issues with anger, her lessons on tough love, and to not be a dummy for nobody. My mom's anger concerned me, and I was glad I found out about God. It was unforgettable. I remember spending time with Him praying about my mom. I used to ask God why my mom was like that.

Our mom was always leaving us with a family member so she could go and live her life. As my older sister grew up, she basically functioned as our mother. She would cook, clean, wash our clothes, and walk with us to school. She would also help us with homework. When it was convenient for my Mom and she wanted to be nice, she would come up to my school and be a part. If we had a party or something and she would bring candy and stuff, that would bring so much joy to my heart.

Things were not stable when I was staying with my mom, and we always moved when we got comfortable at a new house. We always changed schools, and I got so sick and tired of it, but I had to deal with it because I was only a kid. No matter how mom treated me, I always loved her regardless of what went on. At the age of 10, I was taking away from my mom. I had to go to live with my dad. This was the worst time of my life. I had to leave my mom and siblings behind to go stay with my dad and his girlfriend.

At my father's house, it wasn't a bed of roses. His girlfriend was a drug addict. In the middle of the night, she would rob us in our sleep. We would wake up to a letter with our things being gone. I remember every time it was my birthday, my dad would buy me a ring, and I feel so special. But then when his girlfriend went on her binge, she would steal my rings. At the age of ten, I found myself having to miss school and watch after and addict because my father had to go to work to pay the bills. This same woman kept us away from my mother and had me and my sister going to see a therapist, as if we were crazy. Our real issue was that we had a dad that treated someone else's child better than us. Even in the mist of it all, the hand of God was till upon us.

So, when I was in school, I had a hard time with reading and math because no one sat down and taught me anything. I missed school. While attending George Watts Elementary School, I recall meeting a lady named Mrs. Wilson. She was going around to classes to see if students need help with math. Of course, I needed help, so she took me under her wings. She was very helpful in my learning as she simplified everything so that I could understand. She even taught me how to read and spent time with me. I thank God for her she was like a guardian angel for me throughout my life. I thank her for what she did. I thank God He place her in my life.

My dad eventually left his girlfriend as I grew older. But it seemed like trouble never ends. Just when things were looking better, my sister began to get very sick. We always had to take her to the hospital and take her to dialysis because she was born with a kidney problem. It really used to hurt my heart to see her sick. I used to pray for God to heal her as I wanted her to have a normal life. God is a miracle worker; he bought my sister along way. My parents were told that she wasn't going to live past the age 2. I thank God that he spared her life my sister's life about 13 times.

We continued to go to church, and we would pray together as a family. I was still depressed, and one day, my dad nor my sister was home. I got a knife. I put a knife to my wrist, and I begin to cut. Nothing happened. But I thank God that He spared my life because He had a bigger purpose for me even though I didn't understand as a child while I was going through so much, He still had a bigger purpose for me.

Around the age of 15, I began doing very well at school, and I was in the honor society because I made straight A's. My dad made me miss my honor society ceremony because I had to attend an open house to attend private school. It really broke my heart. By this time, I started getting interested in boys. I would connect with them on the chat line and meet them. I had no business meeting up with this people. One day I would get a hard lesson by being the wrong place with the wrong person. I met up with an older guy and he stole my innocence. I tried to explain to him that I wanted to save myself for my husband, and it was my prayer to God. He didn't listen and could care less. My virginity was gone just like that. This led me down a lane I never traveled. I began to sneak boys over. One day, my dad caught me and I will never forget the disappointing look on his face. He told me I had lost all trust with him. This broke my heart. I apologized to him over and over and asked for forgiveness. This drove him to call my aunt, and she said I needed to be raised by a woman. He should have never left me in the house. This caused another transition in my life as I ended up having to move with my cousin. I had to leave my father and my sister. Another painful moment that just broke my heart.

Whoever is reading this, keep your body to yourself because those soul ties are something serious, and you don't know what's going on with your body because you have laid with someone and those spirits came on you. You have to seek God like never before and ask God to break those things off you. Continue to seek healing and stay away from temptations. I thank God for his mercy and his grace because I lived recklessly during my teenage years, but God showed his mercy. He never let me go, so I will forever thank him for that because I could have died. He could have allowed so many things to happen to me, but his love for me was just that much. His arms were around me and not let the world consume me and drag me down to a burning hell. God, I thank you.

I would sometimes pray and talk to God. I would ask him to forgive me and ask why he would allow people to hurt, use, take advantage of me, and just treat me any old kind of way. I have that kind of loving heart, and I was always willing to forgive. I ended up dropping out of high school and enrolling into Durham Tech to get my GED because there were some unfair practices. But I'm glad that no weapon that's formed against me prospered.

As I went to take my test, they couldn't find my name on the roster. I saw them register me twice. I tell you the enemy will use anybody or anyone to block your blessings, especially when it's something inside of you that is great.

He just wanted to try to throw you off your path so you could give up on God's promise.

I met a guy at school and ended up in a domestic violence relationship. He started off sweet and nice until one day he got aggressive with me and put his hands around me to choke me. I was in shock; I never experienced anything like that. I cried in disbelief and pain.

Ladies, always get to really know an individual before you start dating them. Become friends and get to know who that person really is because people can really trick you and set you up to destroy your life, literally. The man ended up apologizing, so I stayed in the relationship. My friends and family didn't like his controlling behaviors toward me. They would say leave him, but I thought I was in love. I ended up getting pregnant by him. The truth really began to come out. On top of being an abuser, he was a liar, cheater, manipulator and who knows what else. Having to deal with all that came with him, I went into premature labor due to stress related issues. It began to affect my body. Our child was born with a father in jail. When he was released, he was his old abusive, cheating self again. The birth of my daughter helped me along my journey.

From there, I eventually got a job and my own place. All to God's glory. I was still in the abusive relationship with a man who started stalking me at work. I ended up pregnant again, and we had a daughter, Honesty. This man's possessiveness of me led him to hurt his own child. Out of jealousy and the time taking care of the children took away from him. I had to work, take care of the household, children, and even him. I don't know why I put up with so much from him. One day, I was dressing my child, and there was a cry from her of pain. I found a bruise that was unexplained. I asked if she had fallen, and he said no. So, I took her to the hospital to find out that her leg was broken. This started a serious of events in my life as social services was now involved. I was under investigation, and it separated me from my children. I had to go through serious things to get them back, which included separating from him, getting a restraining order against him, and so much more. Praise God! I eventually got my kids back.

God, I thank you that you kept me, and you still did not take your hands off of me. You said in your word, you would never leave me nor forsake me. You were always around me when no one else was there. God helped me get through it all. I went back and finished school. I also graduated from phlebotomy class and got certified by the state board. God, I thank you. God I love you. The next year, I left my job at McDonald's and was out of work for a whole 8 months. God sustained me. I ended up getting a job at the hospital for about 5 years and 7 months. I went to school for CNA and got certified.

My mom got sick with cancer, and I had to take care of her, so it put other educational endeavors on hold. Then I lost my grandmother on May 24, 2016. She was my heart and was there all the time. Grandma lived a blessed life for 93 years. May she continue to rest in heaven. After that, my mom ended up passing on July 3, 2016 while I was sitting at her bedside. This took a big toll on me. I literally almost lost my mind. I was in a deep stage of depression as my heart was crushed. I was laying in my bed, and it literally felt like my soul was leaving my body. That's how down and out and depressed I was; I just cried and stayed in a dark room. I eventually lost my job as well. In the process of all of that, my family turned their back on me. I almost lost my life due to losing control of my car.

I told myself I couldn't continue to live like that, or I was going to end up dying. Who was going to be there to take care of my kids? I had to do a reality check. I began to watch pastors on Facebook and began building my relationship with God through fasting and prayer. I started to go back to church. I will never forget the tent meeting on August 5, 2016. I rededicated my life to Christ. I restored my life with the Lord, and he began to restore me from the inside out. My pain became the testimony to push me into purpose. I have a non-profit to help women overcome the adversity in life.

I want to encourage anyone no matter what life may throw at you. You can survive. You must pick yourself up and keep God first. Keep pushing pass the difficulty and sooner or later you will see the fruits of your labor. God will show up and show out. He will turn your ashes into beauty. You will be healed through the process and can't nobody get the glory out of it but God. I want to continue to tell anyone who is reading this book. Try your best at everything you do. Don't listen to what the world tells you. Listen to what God tells you to do. Always keep a relationship with him. Continue to fast and pray for God shall move on your behalf. Do good to people and serve always from the heart. Glorify God in everything you do. Be encouraged. Whatever you are going through, this too shall pass. Through your story, God will get the glory. Your victory over your pain shall be the testimony that helps someone triumph.

SUPPLICATION

Father God,

We come to you right now and ask you to heal every broken and wounded place in our life. God, we surrender it all to you today. We lay it at your feet. God, we ask that your will be done in our life and not our own will. God, we ask you to mold us into the virtuous women you desire. God, you said in your word that we are far more precious than rubies. God, you said you'll never leave us nor forsake us. God, you said you knew us before we were in our mother's womb. You know the journey and plans you have for us.

God, we ask you to break every generational curse. We ask you to break off every wounded area in our life, father God. Help us not to think on the former things but to think on the good things to keep our mind, heart, soul stayed on you. God you will lead us, guide us and protect us. God, we thank you for delivering us, healing us and setting us free. We thank You for using every broken area in our life for purpose. Use it to put us into purpose and to us for your Glory to help people be healed, delivered and set free by the blood of Jesus. We declare and decree it to be so. We thank you for being a right now God. Old things are passed away and behold, all things have become new. God, we know you're going to do it in Jesus name, we pray, Amen. You are the beginning, middle and the end. It is done this day.

AFFIRMATIONS-

I am healed by the stripes of Jesus (Isaiah 53 and 5).

I can do all things through Christ which strengthens me (Philippians 4:13).

Lord, stir up my spirit to do your will (Haggai 1: 14).

I cover myself, my family and my possessions with the blood of Jesus.

I break all spoken curses and negative words that I and others have spoken over my life in Jesus name.

I break and release myself from all generational curses and iniquities as a result of the sins of my ancestors in the name of Jesus.

I forgive any person who has hurt me, disappointed me, abandoned me, mistreated me, or rejected me in the name of Jesus.

The spirit of fear has no power over me because God has given me power, love and a sound mind according to 2 Timothy 1 : 7.

I renounce all ungodly thought patterns, soul ties and belief systems in the name of Jesus.

I renounce all fear, unbelief, and doubt in the name of Jesus.

I renounce all hatred, anger, resentment, revenge, retaliation, offense, unforgiveness, and bitterness in the name of Jesus.

Turn every curse sent my way into a blessing (Nehemiah 13:2).

I cover me, my family and my possessions with the blood of Jesus. No hurt harm or danger can come against us. No weapon formed against us shall prosper.

APPLICATION

Write down a list of things that you are contending with you purpose
Locate scripture in the word of God that deal with the items you listed
Chart your progression in overcoming your obstacles. Write down your struggles, pain, your moment of triumph.

ABOUT THE AUTHOR

Shameka Jones is a mother of two beautiful girls and a native of Durham, North Carolina NC. She had many hardships but, by the word of God and the powerful words of her testimony, she has overcome. Shameka is an overcomer of domestic violence, childhood trauma, generational curses, being overlooked and rejection. She graduated from cornerstone Correspondence Christian School. From there, she became a shift manager, a CNA, a supervisor, EKG trainer, and attended school of ministry. She is an entrepreneur, author, and life coach. Her mission is to help individuals fulfill their purpose in Christ and win souls for the kingdom of God. If you would like to contact Shamika for bookings, or services, please reach out to her by email.

CONTACT INFORMATION

Email Address: ShamekaJones2017@gmail.com

SOCIAL MEDIA

YOU GOT THE GOODS

Dr. Derashay Zorn

She perceives that her merchandise is good, And her lamp does not go out by night. She stretches out her hands to the distaff, And her hand holds the spindle.

Proverbs 31:18-19

Do business until I come. The king says to his servants as he delivers each of them a mina. He supplies them with the resources they need to engage in some form of commerce while he was away. He calls for these ten servants because he trusted them. I also believe that he called upon them because he saw that they had profitable merchandise. He gave all of them the same opportunity and showed no partiality. However, when the king returns he finds out that everyone didn't make the most of the opportunity placed before them. One of the servants was so invested in his merchandise that he yielded an 1000% return, another 500%, and another none. The one who hid his talent and produced nothing was called a wicked servant, and what he had was taken away according to the parable of the Ten Minas as written in Luke 19:11-26.

Just like this king, God has called all of us, given us a talent and provided us with everything we need to generate wealth. When Jesus comes back, what is your account going to look like? Will it be like the servants who produced profits from what they had or the one who produced nothing? I look at the Proverbs 31 woman as the first servant who made 1000% profits from his merchandise. In Proverbs 31:18, we can find some understanding and clarity on why some servants yielded a return and others didn't. Let's take a lesson from the life of this dynamic woman.

YOU HAVE EVERYTHING YOU NEED TO GENERATE WEALTH.

DR. DERASHAY ZORN

The text says that she perceives that her merchandise is good.

Merchandise is goods that one has to buy and sale. Before this woman was able to do any type of business commerce, she had to perceived she had the goods. This means she was consciously aware, understood, or knew that her merchandise was on point. Knowing something gives you the power to operate in your understanding. It gives us the ability to appropriately respond. The scripture tells us that the people of God perish for the lack of knowledge. When we don't know who we are and the merchandise that's on the inside of us, we are perishing. The lack of knowledge puts us in a place of stagnation, confusion, and lack of direction. It keeps us begging for things we already have the ability to possess.

When we don't seek the knowledge of God or reject His knowledge, it keeps us from flourishing in His Kingdom. King Saul rejected the knowledge of God and he became a powerless king. We should seek the knowledge of the kingdom of God because worldly knowledge will destroy us. On the other hand, the wisdom of God leads us in our purpose so that we can move in the place of permission, promise, and prosperity.

The servant who produced nothing with their talent could perceive that they had good merchandise. Even the one that produces at 500% had a limited buy in of the merchandised that they possessed even though they was yielding a return. It reflected through there productivity. We can say a lot of things, but the evidence is in the fruit we bear. It's one thing for someone to believe in you, but it's a game changer when you believe in yourself. Yes, faith without works is still dead. To many dreams are going unfilled because of the lack of working faith and the strong hold of pessimistic views. Negative beliefs will hinder you from utilizing the gift or misuse it. Positive self-perception will cause you to move mountains out of your way to obtain what you believe. What limiting views are keeping you from starting your entrepreneurship endeavor?

On the other hand, the Proverbs 31 Woman had the heart of the first servant. She was able to recognize the merchandise that she produced because she utilized the gifts she had so it could become recognizable by potential customers. Now, she may have not started down the path of entrepreneurship but ended up there as others saw what she did at home for herself and her family. She made garments for herself and her children so that they could be clothed well. When others saw her work, it peeked their interest. They wanted to see if she could make items for them. She took notice of how the market reacted to what she was able to produce. As it became a pattern, something she did for others, a business was produced.

THE WORLD IS WAITING TO PURCHASE YOUR MERCHANDISE

- DR. DERASHAY ZORN

She made the most out of the opportunity. This let me know that she understood what she was gifted to do and she utilized it well. What is a common theme or thing you are assisting or doing for people?

Many people are just doing entrepreneurship endeavors and failing at them. It's not because they don't have good merchandise that they are not successful. The merchandise that they are trying to do commerce with could be perfect but not made for them. That's why it's important to know what God has placed in you. I know because I have wasted many resources on business ventures that were prosperous for other but unsuccessful for myself. I didn't know what my merchandise was, and it was evident in my productivity. However, when I found out what I was gifted at, doing it has generated streams of income for my household.

I'm also reminded of the widow who's debtors was about to come and take her sons in exchange for what she owed them. When she went to the prophet Elisha, he asked her, "What do you have in the house?" And she said, "Your maidservant has nothing in the house but a jar of oil." He told her to go borrow some jars and fill them up with the oil she had at home. She followed the directions, and once all the jars were full, Elisha instructed her to go and sell the oil to pay off her debt and use the rest to live off of with her family. She had her merchandise at home, and it was ready to be consumed.

You have good merchandise the world is waiting on. Its time to be like the woman and follow the instructions God has given us. She was action oriented and therefore was able to produce her merchandise. We have to mobilize ourselves to move in faith so that we can see the results of Gods word for our lives. This widow had to perceive that the oil she had was good. Otherwise, she would have had a difficult time convincing others that her merchandise was good. She could have just seen it as being just oil and unprofitable. This was a common item that she put in the market place and generated income. There are gifts we have, and we look at them as being common. People would love the opportunity to purchase the service or product. We cannot continue to overlook our merchandise God has gifted us with. We don't want to be like the wicked servant in the Bible. Understand, what's common to you is the goldmine that someone is looking to strike. Because it's the solution to their problem.

I remember my first business that has been in operation since 2004 called D' Technology. It is a website and graphic design business that creates corporate identities for businesses. Our slogan is "The One Stop Shop for Your Business Solutions. I was just finishing up my undergrad degree and had started working as the IT Director at a nonprofit agency. My responsibilities were to manage all of the company IT operations. Now, before I came, the company had a web designer who was doing the company website. I'm not sure what happened, but out of nowhere my department had a lack. And it was my responsibility to fill it. We had things on the site that needed to be done. However, my educational background is in computer information system, computer programming, and database design. It had nothing to do with web creation or graphics. Because of the deficiency in my department, I had to do some hands on training and learn how to do website design. Now, I must say that this journey was exciting because of my passion for computers. Thank God for that.

However with learning this new skill I had no clue that it would later birth a business. At that time, I didn't think I was business material. I couldn't perceive that I had the goods. I was fresh out of undergrad and excited to be in a career field I dreamed of as a little girl. I was also happy to work after being a stay at home mom. As I began to develop the corporation websites and marketing materials, others would see it and ask my boss about it. She would then refer them to me. The work was being seen in the market place and it was noticeable to others.

My light was shining, and I had no idea what God was up to. The funny thing about this is at that time I still didn't see that I had the goods. I obtained several business clients from the work, those who my employer knew. Before, I knew it, I was in business and had not established anything. But I had to wake up and begin to perceive that my merchandise was good. And not just good enough to work for somebody but good enough to be its own established entity. Once I understood there was a market for my goods, I finally establish the entity. Even today, that business operates from 95% word of mouth referrals. You never know where this journey will take you when you allow God to lead you by the hand. Now, I help individuals birth or expand in their entrepreneurship endeavors.

Many people live in a framed world, as I previous did, with a mindset that only thought that I was only good enough to be an employee. But I would encourage you to reconsider the mindset. Those same skills you are using to grow someone's else entrepreneurship endeavors are the same ones you can use to build yours. When building our businesses, it doesn't stop us from helping others build there, it just allows us to obtain a greater portion of the revenue that's being circulated in the earth. Therefore, evaluate and examine your merchandise in the market. Finally, establish your business.

I believe in you and KNOW that YOU GOT THE GOODS!!!

SUPPLICATION

Dear God,

I thank you for knitting me together in my mother's womb and providing me with everything I need to become a successful entrepreneur. I repent for not being able to perceive your handiwork beforehand. Father, remove all blind spots, uproot every evil seed, and destroy every strong hold of hinderance upon me in the name of Jesus. I thank you for the awakening in my spirit and the opening of my eyes, heart, and mind so I may know that I am fearfully and wonderfully made. You are an awesome, God. Thanks for showing me the good merchandise I hold.

I ask that you may guide me according to your word so that it will be utilize in the fullness of your capacity. I'm taking a stand today to be a city on the hill that cannot be hidden, so when other see my good works, you may be glorified in the name of Jesus. Never again will I hide my talents from being used for your glory. I thank you in advance for the increase that it will cause in my life and others. I know full well that you have given me this gift that it may be unto the servant hood of others. Because of you, I am. Without you, I would be nothing. Therefore, let your word shine forth in my life like the day breaks forth in the morning, that it may bring light to all that's under it and display your glory in the name of Jesus. May I run with the vision that you have for my life as the gazelle runs through the fields. It is you I seek to bring glory and honor. I commit all my ways unto you so that every entrepreneurship venture shall be proper in the name of Jesus. I'm so grateful for all that you are doing in my life. As I embrace my new journey, I know that I will enjoy every step of the way with you.

AFFIRMATION

I have good merchandise.
I am the solution to someone else's problem.
My skills and gifts are profitable.
The world is looking for the merchandise I carry.
I shall move forward in the spirit of entrepreneurship.
The works of my hands are blessed.
Everything I tread upon shall be given unto me.
I am a success.
I am prosperous.
I am gifted.
I am useful.
I shall use my gifts to help others.
God shall get the glory from my gift.

APPLICATION

I Got The Goods!!!

What is your merchandise? Write a list of the things you are good at doing and/or what areas do you assist others with the most?

List the type of business opportunities that can be developed based upon what you are good at doing. Ex. *If you are good at designing graphics, then a business development opportunity could be a graphic designer.*

Merchandise: Gifted to Do   Business Opportunities

_____   _____

_____   _____

_____   _____

Examine your merchandise in the market.

Take on one of the business ventures and develop a vision for it. Once the vision is developed then begin to run.

Run tell that: Begin to talk about your business venture and begin to spread the word. Do some pro bono or sample work. Write down a list of individuals or entities that could utilize your services. Pitch to individuals just to test your market. Don't pitch to the corporations until you have a legal entity and have all your branding in order. However, you have a vision to pitch your service to them.

Individuals

_____   _____

_____   _____

_____   _____

_____   _____

_____   _____

Now that you see you have the goods, get the business established.

ABOUT THE AUTHOR

Kingdom Strategist, Blueprint Builder, and Spiritual Midwife, **Dr. Derashay Zorn** is an international business coach and expert in the art of **unleashing purpose, developing dreams, and expanding untapped potentials within individuals, corporations, and ministries.** Her passion for information technology has led her to obtain a Master of Science in Information System Management which equipped her to **specialize in analyzing, developing and managing systems to birth or expand individuals and entities into the next dimension of kingdom implementation.**

Derashay equips mankind globally as the Founder of the **Kingdom Influencers Network, In The Church™ TV & Radio Broadcast, Divine Order Restoration Ministries (D.O.R.M) International, Kingdom Strategist Firm, Women of Influence Magazine, (D.O.R.M) Publishing** and many other entrepreneurship endeavors that equip mankind globally. Through her global brands **Kingdom Strategies University® & School of Authorpreneur®**, she teaches others **how to maximize their potential and monetize their gifts and talents** as a critical vehicle for fulfilling their purpose, making a significant impact and branding influence that can instantly and beautifully change the world. Her books and workbook titled **"Abortions In the Church: Divine Strategies to Spiritual Deliverance" & Meant for My Good: Being Developed in The Midst of the Disaster** is helping others overcome and give birth to their purpose, visions, and dreams. She is a wife, mother, pastor, entrepreneur; consultant, empowerment speaker, mentor, and friend.

Her philosophy is **"A critical tool for self-development is learning how to cultivate, build and release others into their destinies."**

CONTACT INFORMATION

Email Address: info@derashayzorn.com

Website: www.derashayzorn.com

SOCIAL MEDIA

Twitter: @kbstrategist

Facebook Page: @kingdomstrategist

Instagram:: @kingdomstrategist

I AM THAT WOMAN
Dr. Jeri B. Shannon

Proverbs 31:10

I can remember, as a little girl, I used to dream about what life would be like when I grew up. I had my husband picked out, my beautiful children, my house and even my cars. Yes, I had it all mapped out.

Until one day I woke up single with four kids and nothing I dreamed about came true. I was divorced, depressed and my dream house and dream husband was out the door.

When I look back over my life, I would say nothing went as planned until I took a look into the mirror and saw who I had become. I was a girl who wanted the whole world but didn't know how to get it. I had a big dream but no tools nor direction on how to get there.

Have you ever felt like giving up, but there was something on the inside said keep going, don't stop? Yes, this is my story, a single mother with four beautiful children with a dream.

One day I woke up. You would ask, "What do you mean, you woke up?" I fell in LOVE with Jesus and it meant the world to me. That's when I realized I was that woman they were talking about in Proverbs 31.

I am that woman, the woman who serves her God with love and passion. I am the woman who captures God's attention with her ways and heart. Who is this woman that virtuous man can find?

That woman is You.

Yes, that woman is you, the one they said would never amount to anything. The one who had her baby out of wedlock, yes that's you. The one who was on drugs and alcohol and was selling her body to get another hit. The one who never got an education, yes that's you. You are that woman.

Say it, **I AM THAT WOMAN!**

You are that masterpiece, who God has created to be. You are that woman who looks into the mirror and see the pain, tears, hurt, joy and love that is all part of you. You can erase the past, but we sure learn from them. I know I sure did.

When I took a look at that woman, I found out that she has a heart for her husband and she's not married yet; she pours her heart into her father which is in heaven. She spends time with the master, not only to ask of need or want but to get to know him in a more intimate way. She loves on him and makes Him feel special and she knows how.

That woman also works good with her hands, you see a proverbs 31 woman is really a business woman. She's like a merchant who brings her food from a far. This woman knows how to run her household and love her family.

Your price is above rubies…. Do you know how much rubies cost? Well from what I've researched, one carat is over one million dollars. Now, let's talk about self worth. We are above rubies, that tells us that we are priceless. There was a time in my life when I didn't have self worth nor did I even know what that even meant. I always wanted more and took a stand on what I wanted but still didn't know my worth.

There is a scripture that says:

1 Corinthians 13:11, "When I was a child, I spake as a child, I understood as a child, I thought as a child: but when I became a man, I put away childish things."

I can remember when I was younger and didn't know my worth; I understood as a child, I thought as a child, and I did childish things. But when I became an adult and begin to really see what life had to offer me and not only that but begin to get personal development into my life. My whole thought pattern changed. Don't you know, even as an adult, we still can think childishly, until I started listening to others who knew more than me and had the lifestyle to prove it. I stopped and looked into the mirror and said, "Jeri, what are you doing to yourself?"

I said to myself, "Jeri, you deserve more than what you are getting and it's about time you start doing the work and start working on yourself." Listen, I've been spoiled all my life. My grandfather spoiled me, and then I met men who spoiled me. Yes, I'm married to a wonderful man right now who would give me my heart's desires and that was a God thing. But back to me, because I've been spoiled I became selfish and really had to work on me.

I thought I knew myself worth but really didn't know a thing. I was working on selfishness. Anybody know about that? Selfishness, greed, and spoiled are all in the same category. When I began to do the work and take one personal development, I found out the little girl didn't have it all together.

Knowing your worth is taking a look into the mirror and asking yourself, WHO AM I? That's when you get to the bottom of being that woman that God designed from the beginning of time. Knowing your worth is more than money, Louis Vuitton, coach bags, Gucci, Christian Diors and all the name brands that we sometime feel we need to feel like we are worth something.

The word says you're more valuable than rubies, and the last time I checked, rubies are worth more than hand bags.

She is beautiful in every way; her smile, her lips, hips and finger tips makes her distant. There is no one like her. God made you unique and special. Remember this, when God made you, everything was made before you came on the scene. God wanted things set and in order before He made the Queen of the universe. Wow ladies, you are one of a kind. To the point, when Adam looked at you, he said, "WOW." Yes, that's what he said then he called you WOMAN.

That woman will work willingly with her hands Yes she works willingly with her hands and takes care of her family. That woman has no problem going out into the field to bring meat to her household. She is the encourager and the worker. She makes her man want to go out and provide for his family, yes she's just that good, she knows how to keep her home together and everyone is in harmony.

The Proverbs 31 virtuous woman is a business woman. She was like a merchant where she managed her house like a business. She assigned tasks to her handmaids and managed her house with profits.

You are that woman who equips herself with strength spiritual, mental, and physical fitness for her God-given task and makes her arms strong.

NOW THE LORD HAD SAID UNTO ABRAM, GET THEE OUT OF THY COUNTRY, AND FROM THY KINDRED, AND FROM THY FATHER'S HOUSE, UNTO A LAND THAT I WILL SHEW THEE: GENESIS 12:1

Now, let me tell you about a woman who left her family to obey God. She was sold out for God, and one day the Lord spoke in prayer and said move to California. This woman has four teenage children and no money. She waited until God said, "Now is the time." She went and brought a brand new car, which was the hand of the Lord on her life for her to even buy a car in her name because of her credit. That was a miracle in itself, but she obeyed God.

After she brought the car, the Lord said, "Now is the time to move to Los Angeles, CA," and she obeyed. Once she got her with a friend who helped her drive, they really didn't have much money. For a matter of fact, she had about $200 to her name and her friend helped with gas. The Lord ordered her steps. Once they got to Los Angeles, her friend remembered, she had some friends living there. She called them and they invited us to their home and let us stay for two weeks. After the two weeks were over, she asked what I was going to do. She said let's pray. After prayer, the Lord spoke and said, I didn't tell you to visit; I told you to move.

Once she decided she was not going back home, God opened a door to get an apartment the same day from her friends who manage the apartments they lived in. Keep in mind she had no money, so she got the apartment without any money. After living there for a couple of months, the Lord spoke to her and said move to Los Angeles because where she lived was about an hour away from Los Angeles. She started going through her wallet and saw a business card she had from a man who lived in Los Angeles she meet three years prior. God spoke to her and told her to call him. When she told him she lived there in California, far out in the Rancho Cucamonga area, but was thinking about moving into Los Angeles.

This gentleman requested to come pick her up and take her to the safe parts of LA to look at some apartments and she agreed. Once going to look at apartments, that's when she got a wakeup call about how much it costs to live in LA. She began to wonder how she would get her kids there. Again, God was right there by her side. As she stares out the window, the gentleman asked what was she thinking about, and she didn't want to tell him she was thinking about how expensive it is in California; so she said oh nothing. He asked, are you thinking about how expensive it was out here, and she said yes. He explained, "It's very expensive to live out here but I'll tell you what I'm going to do." The gentleman said, "I'll move out of my condo and let you move in, and I'll go stay with my girlfriend."

Wow, the woman said, "You will do that for me, and he said these words, "You are a woman of God aren't you." She answered, yes. That day her life changed. He set a date to move her things into his place, and he moved in with his girlfriend just like he promised. A total stranger gave over his keys and condo to a woman of God. She stayed there for six months, and the gentleman respected. He never asked when she was moving; he just asked her to get his mail and he'll pick it up once a week. The gentleman was a Caucasian, and he never confessed that he was a believer but what he did told her he was. He was an angle sent by God to make sure she was taken care of. She didn't pay rent not utilities to the place; she just moved in.

On her first job interview in Los Angeles, she met her husband. He hired her and God proved to her He was with her all the way and now she's living a dream. That woman I must say is ME. God did it for me only because I obeyed and trust HIM through it all. I told God I will tell my story till my last breath because I give Him all the Glory and all the praise.

There is a happily ever after story and they do exist, are you willing to be that woman that God designed. Stop looking outside and look within. Say it I AM THAT WOMAN" say it again "I AM THAT WOMAN." Be that woman that God wants you to be. Live out your best life.

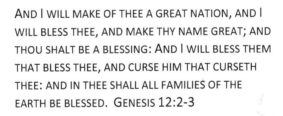

AND I WILL MAKE OF THEE A GREAT NATION, AND I WILL BLESS THEE, AND MAKE THY NAME GREAT; AND THOU SHALT BE A BLESSING: AND I WILL BLESS THEM THAT BLESS THEE, AND CURSE HIM THAT CURSETH THEE: AND IN THEE SHALL ALL FAMILIES OF THE EARTH BE BLESSED. GENESIS 12:2-3

SUPPLICATIONS

Father, in the name of Jesus. I thank you for this opportunity to pray and be heard by millions. I pray first that your hand be upon us and that you will give us the wisdom to do your will. I proclaim I am set free, and no weapon form against us shall prosper and every tongue that rise up against us shall be brought into judgment. Father, I pray that every woman reading this book will be encouraged to obey you in every way. Father, I call those things which be not as though they were. So call everyone who is reading this pray healed, delivered and set free. I also pray for my sisters who are still struggling with identifying who they are; I pray a hedge of protection around them, Lord, and that you would guide them to all truth just like you did me and others.

AFFIRMATIONS

I AM THAT WOMAN.

I am the head and not the tail.

I am more than a conqueror through Christ who strengthens me.

I am beautiful

I am prosperous.

I am gifted & whole.

I am Blessed.

Everything my hand's touch shall prosper.

I am a Millionaire.

It is my divine right as a child of God to be showered with luxurious wealth, riches and magnificent success.

APPLICATION

I take a stand on what I believe in, and God has given me a gift to empower others and nothing can stop me. There was a time when I felt like I was not educated enough, smart enough, or cute enough. But, today is a different day. I took a stand and took my life back from the devil. The devil told me all those things, but today I stand firm on what God said I AM, and it is settled in heaven. Ladies, stand firm on what God said you are and NEVER give up on your dreams and passion.

It all starts with a decision to take a stand then you move upon it. Right now say, "I can and I will!!!" Say it with me **"I WILL NEVER GIVE UP."**

ABOUT THE AUTHOR

Dr. Jeri B. Shannon, A dedicated champion of women, Jeri has devoted her career to advancing and supporting women in the pursuit of their dreams. Thousands of women from executive leaders, administrative assistants and moms returning to the workforce have benefited from Jeri's unique guidance on how to maximize life success. She finds that spark within each of us and turns it into a fire.

Jeri has become a bestselling author, a renowned speaker, business owner, mentor and community leader of various sectors of the community. Jeri is active in causes relating to women and girls around the country.

Jeri made millions working from home selling office supplies to the federal government. She has a keen way of turning everything she touches into gold. With her experience, she had to overcome obstacles and personal struggles as a young single mother to achieve her destiny. Dedicated to facilitating the growth and evolution of human consciousness; she continues to reach within the soul and bring out the best in mankind. Jeri mentors women across the nation, and she speaks straight-from-the-heart. Dr. Shannon currently Co-Pastors with her husband, Apostle Anthony Shannon at **"Stand & Be Counted Worship Center"** in Los Angeles, California. She's the visionary of **"I AM THAT WOMAN TOUR"**, owns several businesses, a renowned professional speaker, author, and Talk Show. One of Jeri's famous quotes of **"Whatever the Lord Says about It" "With the Quickness,"** Hallelujah, and **"Plant you now and dig you later"**.

CONTACT INFORMATION

Email Address: info@jerishannon.com

Website: www.jerishannon.com

SOCIAL MEDIA

Twitter: @jerishannon

Facebook Page: @jerishannon

Instagram: @jerishannon

CONTACT DR. DERASHAY ZORN

FOR BOOKING CONTACT DR. ZORN AT

www.derashayzorn.com or info@derashayzorn.com

AVAILABLE TITLES

IF YOU ENJOYED THIS BOOK, HERE ARE OTHER DR. ZORN BOOKS AVAILABLE ON AMAZON:

Abortions In The Church: Divine Strategies to Spiritual Deliverance Book

Abortions In The Church: Divine Strategies to Spiritual Deliverance Workbook

Meant for My Good: Being Developed in the Midst of the Disaster Anthology

Parentpreneur Success Guide – Co Author Edition

COMING FALL 2019

31 Ways of Influence

Delivering My Expectation

The Rules of Success

COMING IN 2020

Influence 365

40: The Wilderness Experience Survival Guide – Entrepreneurship Edition

31 Ways of Influence: Volume 2

I AM H.E.R. Collective Series

Made in the USA
Lexington, KY
06 December 2019